With best
wishes,

CREDITS

Editor
Arvel Gray

Research assistance
Craig Loewen
Lindsay Lovallo

Design and layout
Dawn Huck

Associate editors
Barbara Huck
Peter St. John
Deborah Riley

Prepress and printing
Friesens, Canada

Front cover images: The Liberal government of John Bracken on the Manitoba Legislature steps about 1922. Photo courtesy of the Liberal Party of Manitoba.

Senator Sharon Carstairs and Jon Gerrard with young Liberal members at an annual general meeting in River Heights, March 2006. Photo by Ruslan Tracz.

Back cover images: For decades, Manitoba's legislative sessions ended with paper fight; this one took place about 1950, under Premier Douglas Campbell. Photo courtesy of the Liberal Party of Manitoba.

Author Jon Gerrard at one of the northern lakes he loves. Photo courtesy of the Gerrard Family.

Library and Archives Canada Cataloguing in Publication

Gerrard, Jon, 1947-

    Battling for a better Manitoba : a history of the provincial Liberal Party / Jon Gerrard ; with Gary Girard.

ISBN 1-896150-31-4

    1. Liberal Party in Manitoba--History. 2. Manitoba--Politics and government. I. Girard, Gary II. Title.

JL299.A53G47 2006   324.27127'06   C2006-411-6

Conseil des Arts   Canada Council
du Canada   for the Arts

We gratefully acknowledge the support of the Canada Council for the Arts.

We are also grateful for the continuing support and encouragement of Manitoba Culture, Heritage and Tourism.

BATTLING FOR A BETTER MANITOBA

A History
of the Provincial Liberal Party

By Jon Gerrard
with Gary Girard

Heartland Associates, Inc.
Winnipeg, Canada

Printed in Manitoba, Canada

Table of Contents

Acknowledgements

I THANK MY FAMILY—my wife Naomi, my three children Pauline, Charles, and Thomas, my son-in-law Roger, and my parents John and Betty—for enabling me to have the privilege of serving in political life. It has not always been easy for them—and for those difficulties I apologize.

I thank the members who chose me as leader, and for those who participated in the competitive process through their support for Jerry Fontaine. It has been a privilege to serve as Liberal leader.

I thank the members of the Liberal Party in Manitoba who have continued to provide support for me and active debate and concern about the future of Manitoba. In particular, I am grateful to the several presidents with whom I have had the privilege of working while I have been leader. These include Zella Vermeulen, John Scurfield, Gordon Kirkby, Val Thompson, Dennis Dempsey and Warren Thompson. Each has played a very important role in building and shaping our party. I am also very grateful to the many executive, board members and staff who have contributed their time, their talents and considerable efforts to make sure the Manitoba Liberal Party is run well and is in good financial shape. I am grateful as well to the many constituency presidents and their executives. Members of local constituency associations have made a huge contribution to the party and to me as leader—providing a constant stream of advice and suggestions, helping to organize meetings and events when I visited the constituency, and ensuring we have continuing vigorous annual meetings.

I would like to say a particular thanks to individuals who have served as political mentors to me—Lloyd Axworthy, Sharon Carstairs, Gildas Molgat, Paul Edwards, Jean Chrétien and John Manley.

Thanks are also owed to many who helped in gathering material for this book, or contributed to its production, including especially Alana McKenzie and Jane Nikkel, who served as my executive assistants from 1999–2004. I am particularly grateful to Arvel Gray, who did a fabulous job of editing, and to Barbara Huck, Peter St. John, Dawn Huck and Lindsay Lovallo at Heartland Associates who have worked so hard to produce this book.

Many others helped me gather materials, or read through and provided helpful comments on the book. Rhonda Gordon, Kevin Wynne, Sharon Jones, Sean Petty and Chris Petty each went through the manuscript very thoroughly at one point or another during the book's development. Many others including Bertrand Boily, Doris Au, Frank McKendry, Campbell Wright, Rhonda Gordon, Dennis Dempsey, Kevin Lamoureux, Carie Willson, Allan Mills, Morris Mott, Bernie Wolfe, Marvin Krawec, Don McIntosh, Paul Edwards, Meryle Lewis, Ruslan Tracz, Ted Klassen, Dennis Trochim, Craig Loewen, Shane Sadorski and Leah Ross also contributed. To all of you, I say thank you. Your help and guidance have been much appreciated.

Jon Gerrard
March 2006

Preface

JON GERRARD SEEMS TO LIKE DAUNTING TASKS. He has been
a cancer researcher, a federal minister of Science, Research and
Development and, for the last several years, leader of the provincial
Liberal Party in Manitoba—activities which each in its own way
have kept him out on the edge.

He has now added to this portfolio of intrepid initiatives the
writing of a history of the Manitoba Liberal Party—a daunting task
indeed. But for adherents to the party, and there is still a cohort
of loyal followers, as well as those who relish a good political tale,
this is an informative read.

This book is clearly a labour of love. Gerrard brings immense
patience, fortitude and affection to his narrative, which outlines
the vicissitudes in fortune of this political party. This is a party
that has gone from being a dominant force in the province to its
present minority status. He recounts the achievements and near
misses of some of the giants of public policy in the province—
Sifton, Norris, Garson, Campbell and, in more contemporary
times, Molgat and Asper. He also carefully records the contributions of lesser-known Liberal leaders such as Bobby Bend, Charles
Huband, Doug Lauchlan and Paul Edwards, all of whom displayed
integrity and conscience. Also included are many stalwart MLAs
who brought colour and verve to the legislature.

There is the exciting interlude in the late 1980s when, under
the leadership of Sharon Carstairs, there was a resurgence in public
support resulting in the party regaining status as the province's
official opposition. This opened up opportunity in the legislative
chamber for a lively and talented group of MLAs, only to have
them fall from grace again over the great constitutional divide of
Meech Lake.

Gerrard reminds us of some of the notable Liberal accomplishments in setting progressive agendas for the province. He pays
special attention to the social and women's rights achievements

of the Norris government and the electrification of the rural areas under D.L. Campbell, which brought parity to the rural regions.

I recall my own entry to the legislature in 1973 for the downtown riding of Fort Rouge; our small caucus of three members became the voice of urban issues in a house mainly dominated by the concerns of rural representatives. This was a crossroads moment for the Liberal Party and indeed for the province as we were being led by Israel Asper. "Izzy" brought his prodigious talents and energy to setting out an economic development blueprint that envisioned capitalizing on our energy and human resources, and seeing Winnipeg as an international hub of enterprise and development.

It may seem trite to say it was ahead of its time. And it was clearly not a grabber with the voters. But if Asper had been able to establish a respectable beachhead in the legislature from which he could have eventually become the government then there might have been a very different future for the province. On second thought, maybe his defeat was all to the good, for he went on to build a communications empire that brought its related economic and philanthropic weight to the benefit of Manitobans.

What Asper faced, and what continues to be the bane of successive Liberal leaders, was the equivalent of a political double whammy. First, is the inherent bi-polarity of provincial politics where the conservatives hold strong bastions in the southern farming areas and the well-to-do suburbs of Winnipeg and the NDP have equally strong redoubts in Northern Manitoba, the Interlake and Winnipeg's North End. The government prize goes to either of those two parties that can capture the swing areas of Winnipeg and a few seats in Brandon by appealing to liberals; much as Gary Doer does today.

Then there is the problem of the eight-hundred pound gorilla, more fondly known as the federal Liberals, which has been the most successful political machine in the Western world (even taking into account the somewhat spotty record of the past few years). "The feds", as they are called in provincial party circles, have caused and will continue to cause no end of trouble for their provincial cousins. They have a record of making unpopular decisions usually at inopportune moments. Asper's 1973 campaign was seriously undermined by a federal budget that raised taxes, for example.

Another serious effect is the Ottawa brain drain. In a small province there is only a limited quantum of men and women who will run for office, contribute to a campaign, and become poll workers. That quantum gets divided amongst the various parties and is further subdivided between federal and provincial wings—though there are many who do double duty. In the case of the Manitoba Liberals, the attraction to becoming an active "fed", with the possibility of holding office, achieving policy results, and somewhat more crassly, gaining appointments, honours and acknowledgement, often works to the disadvantage of the provincial party. I know whereof I speak.

Gerrard recognizes this problem, having been a federal MP, and has gone about rectifying the structural impediments by splitting the party apparatus into two distinct organizations and building his own team of dedicated supporters.

He may also be riding the wave of some good fortune because of the defeat of the federal Liberals in the last election. There will be a period of rebuilding and leadership contestation. But there will not be the attraction of power that has drawn so many Manitoba Liberals to the federal scene for so long. This is a good time to focus on provincial issues and prospects.

This book will serve as a useful instruction for those searching for meaning, depth and continuity in their political leadership. The disgraceful example of David Emerson's recent political bed hopping and the emergence of a class of ersatz putative liberal leaders at the federal level bring home the need to establish roots and to use history as a guide.

Jon Gerrard has not only given us a book of interest in the political evolution of our province, he may have given himself a talisman to attract voters to a homegrown, made in Manitoba, legitimate expression of liberalism.

> The Hon. Lloyd Axworthy
> President, The University of Winnipeg

Dr. Jon Gerrard

1

Why, Why, Why Consider Leaving Medicine?

On a bright, sunny day in late summer of 1992, when I was a member of the Faculty of Medicine at the University of Manitoba, I sat down with the Dean of Medicine, Dr. Nick Anthonisen, and explained my intention to run for political office. Dr. Anthonisen's response was immediate: "Why, why, why would you consider leaving medicine? You have a great career as a scientist and a physician. Why are you even thinking about going into politics?"

I knew why. Our health care system was at risk and we needed changes in science and health care that could only be made at the political level. I wanted to see what I could do.

Dr. Anthonisen put up all sorts of arguments—it was a waste of time, there was little chance of me being elected, and even less chance of being able to influence events. I knew full well that I might not even succeed in getting the nomination to run as a candidate, but being a determined sort, my mind was made up.

As it happened, I was successful in receiving the Liberal nomination in Portage-Interlake in the fall of 1992. I was successful in being elected the member of Parliament for Portage-Interlake in October 1993. Shortly afterwards, I was sworn into the first cabinet of Prime Minister Jean Chrétien as the Secretary of State for Science, Research and Development, and in January 1996, I was given the added responsibility for Western Economic Diversification.

Following my defeat in the federal election of 1997, I moved into provincial politics; in the fall of 1998, I became the Liberal leader in Manitoba. I thought I knew what I was getting into, but I had a great deal to learn, indeed, more than I would have dreamed possible when I began. Jim Millar, a friend and fellow Liberal from the Interlake, had warned me that it would be totally different from federal politics. I later came to appreciate how accurate he was.

Fundamentally, the Manitoba Liberal Party believes in fiscal responsibility and social justice—understanding and providing for those in our society most in need. The party is concerned with improving the provincial government and democracy, and has consistently fought for innovation and for new ideas—to ensure Manitoba a place in the changing world. The party believes in diversity and has fought to bridge the rural-urban divide, to build successful rural as well as urban economies and communities.

Provincial Liberals value the need for individual initiative and entrepreneurship and understand how the apparently conflicting concepts of competition and cooperation can be mutually complementary.

The Liberal party was based on the traditions of Canadian and international liberalism, but I remember an eye-opening conversation I once had with a young student who asked, "But your party does not really have a philosophy, does it?" I realized not everyone saw or understood the values and ideas that are the foundation of the party, or knew its history, which is rooted in the birth of our province, and includes four Liberal premiers and years of innovative, yet fiscally responsible Liberal governments.

This book is the story of the Manitoba Liberal Party. It is the story of men and women who put aside their careers as farmers, auctioneers, lawyers, teachers, doctors and entrepreneurs to improve the lives of the citizens of this province. It is a story of courage and triumph.

A great number of the party's political pioneers were instrumental in establishing many of the rights and institutions Manitobans now take for granted. Thomas Greenway, a storekeeper from Ontario who led a large party of settlers to establish Crystal City in southern Manitoba, spent ten years building the provincial Liberal Party before he became premier. His drive to increase immigration to Manitoba, to increase competition in the railways, to improve agricultural efforts and to institute a province-wide school system, laid important foundations for the province.

Tobias Norris, a farmer and auctioneer from western

Manitoba, doggedly built the Liberal Party and restored confidence in government at a time when widespread corruption had undermined faith in elected officials. His government has been widely acknowledged as one of the most progressive and reformist governments in Manitoba's history.

Stuart Garson practised law in the Interlake before being elected as the local MLA in 1928. When he became premier in 1943, he led the way in working with the federal government to put in place Canada's first Equalization Transfer Program, affording Manitoba better opportunities.

D. L. Campbell, a farmer from the Portage area who spent twenty-six years in politics before becoming premier, positioned Manitoba for prosperity and strong economic growth in the 1950s.

Even in opposition, the party has been visionary in building Manitoba and in bridging the nation's east-west divide. During his tenure as Liberal leader, entrepreneur Israel Asper demonstrated his ability to think big to secure our future. Sharon Carstairs, the first woman in Canada to hold the title of leader of the Official Opposition, led the way in urging for dramatically increased spending on innovation and research.

The Manitoba Liberal Party has occupied the centre of the political spectrum in the province, just as Manitoba has been at the centre of the Canadian federation. At times, the party has served as a conscience, offering the voice of reason and tolerance. Its presence and its leaders have been likened to the keystone— a constant reminder to the other two parties that there is an innovative, forward-thinking middle way.

While there are those who have become dispirited as a result of lost elections, there is much to be proud of. Like provincial politics itself, researching and writing this book has been a voyage of discovery. My hope is that this work acknowledges the legacy of the men and women who nurtured the party from its infancy to the twenty-first century, and becomes a proud reminder of what is achievable in our future.

Louis Riel, the man many call the true father of Manitoba

2

The God Who Speaks
Before 1888

*"... [I]t is considered proper that the province which is to
be organized shall be called Manitoba ... an old Indian
name, meaning 'the god who speaks' ..."*
Prime Minister John A. Macdonald
Speaking on the Manitoba Act, May 2, 1870[1]

WHETHER OR NOT ONE ACCEPTS THE TRANSLATION of "Manitoba"
provided by Canada's first prime minister, no one can deny that
the province was believed to be a place of the Great Spirit, the
Creator. The name Manito-ba—the place where the Great Spirit
speaks—may have been given first to an island just north of the
narrows on Lake Manitoba. At this site, certain conditions of
wind and water give rise to sounds which are similar to whisper-
ing or speaking. Over time, the name was extended to the whole
of Lake Manitoba, and eventually to the entire province.

From its earliest days, Manitoba was an important meeting
place. Centuries before Europeans arrived, during a cycle of global
warming that climatologists call the Medieval Warm Period, many
of the cultures of North America's Great Plains were beset by

---

[1] House of Commons of Canada, Dominion Debates, 1870, vol 1: 1287–1320—
referenced in Frances Russell, *The Canadian Crucible*. (Heartland Associates Inc.,
Winnipeg, 2003) p. 88. The origin of the name, Manitoba, has been the subject of
debate. In Cree or Ojibwe, it means 'the strait of the Great Spirit'—believed to refer to
the narrows of Lake Manitoba and the roar of the waters moving through this passage.
(Ham, Penny: *Place Names of Manitoba*, (Western Producer Prairie Books, 1980)

drought and starvation. But in Manitoba, food was abundant, and the nations were at peace. The Cree from the boreal forest and the Anishinabe (or Ojibwe) from the lake regions to the east shared the land with the Siouan-speaking Nakota (or Assiniboine) from the south, travelling seasonally to hunt and trade. About 700 years ago, as hunger and desperation turned to warfare in the south, as many as nine different nations gathered for a great Peace Meeting at the confluence of the Red and Assiniboine Rivers. Predating the founding of the Five Nations Iroquois by centuries, it was perhaps the world's first effort to find peace through multinational dialogue.

Archaeological evidence also shows that relatives of the Oneota, a corn-growing Mississippi River culture, had settled at Lockport, on the lower Red River, by about 600 years ago.

About three centuries later, in the late 1600s, English-speaking fur traders established posts on the shores of Hudson Bay, but other than occasional trips inland, they were content to remain by the bay, awaiting the large Cree and Nakota delegations that annually arrived to trade. Beginning in the 1720s, however, French-speaking voyageurs, accompanied by Anishinabe guides and hunters, began making the long journey from the St. Lawrence to trade in the camps and villages of aboriginal Manitobans. By the early 1800s, the Montréal-based fur traders, who had amalgamated to form the North West Company, dominated the region surrounding what is now Winnipeg.

The Hudson's Bay Company claimed title to the land, however, and in 1812 a Scottish earl, Lord Selkirk, arrived with settlers, intent on developing a settlement along the Red River. Not surprisingly, there was conflict between the newcomers and the voyageurs and merchants of the North West Company, but in 1821 the rival companies merged; soon the fledgling settlements along the Red River became the HBC's Western Canadian headquarters. With grand forts first at Lower Fort Garry and later at Upper Fort Garry—later to become Winnipeg—Manitoba was ruled for many years by the company's governor, George Simpson, dubbed "the little Emperor".

The settlements grew slowly and, as they had for centuries, the many European traders married Cree, Anishinabe and Nakota women and their Métis, or mixed-blood, offspring became a dominant force in the province. For more than fifty years, life in Manitoba developed with a relative balance among First Nations communities, the Scottish and Orcadian mixed-blood settlements of the Hudson's Bay Company, and a growing number of Métis villages peopled by offspring of the francophone traders of the North West Company.

As the nineteenth century waned, however, a clash of these cultures set the stage for the birth of Canada's fifth province and provided the genesis of our early government and legislative activity. The trouble began in 1869, when the whole of Rupert's Land (the enormous tract of land draining into Hudson Bay, which had been chartered, sight unseen, to the Hudson's Bay Company two centuries before) was to be transferred to the infant nation of Canada. Surveyors arrived and began to assess the land based on mile square sections. These new borders severed many existing boundaries of the long, narrow river lots that had been established long before by the Métis. Young Louis Riel and his fellow Métis stopped the survey, took possession of Upper Fort Garry and, following negotiations with the English-speaking colonists, an elected provisional government was established by Riel. The fledgling government's representatives travelled east to Ottawa, where negotiations with Prime Minister Macdonald led to acknowledgement of the rights of the Métis and the development of the terms of the Manitoba Act to establish Manitoba as a province of Canada.

In the spring of 1870, when the Manitoba Act was debated in the House of Commons, the province had approximately equal numbers of those whose recorded primary language was French and those who spoke English. A census taken in the tiny original "postage stamp" province of Manitoba also showed the predominance of the Métis or mixed-blood citizens (eighty-two per cent) and recorded 558 people whose first language was Cree, Anishinabe or Sioux. [2]

Adams Archibald, a member of Parliament from Nova Scotia, emphasized in his speech that the bill should be seen as a "deed of partnership between French and English Canadians in the development of the North West." [3]

George Etienne Cartier, the deputy prime minister, spoke to convey his belief that the province of Manitoba was the "key" to the future of the whole of Western Canada. "May the inhabitants of the new province always speak to the inhabitants of the North West the language of reason, truth and justice," he declared.

Alexander Mackenzie, the leader of the Liberal opposition rose to ask why the important community of Portage la Prairie had

[2] John Welsted, John Everitt, John and Christoph Stadel, *The Geography of Manitoba.* (The University of Manitoba Press, 1996) p. 127.

[3] Frances Russell, *The Canadian Crucible,* (Heartland Associates Inc., Winnipeg, 2003) p. 90.

been excluded from the new province. In response, an amendment was brought in and so Portage la Prairie became part of the tiny province, still only one-eighteenth of its current size.

On May 12, 1870, the Manitoba Act was passed by the Canadian Parliament, by a vote of 120 to eleven. On June 23rd, the land was transferred from the Hudson's Bay Company to the Government of Canada and the following day, the Manitoba Act was endorsed by Riel's provisional government, which had largely achieved the demands it had made to Ottawa, including the protection of Métis' lands and the use of the French language in the Legislature and the courts. The Manitoba Act was finally proclaimed on July 15, 1870, officially creating the new province.

Unofficially, the act also made Louis Riel Manitoba's first *de facto* premier, acknowledging him as head of the provisional government until August 24, 1870, when Colonel Garnet Wolseley and his troops arrived in Winnipeg, ostensibly to maintain order and keep the peace.

In establishing their authority, Louis Riel and the provisional government had executed Thomas Scott, an Irish-born Canadian who had resisted Riel's government and fought against him in the Red River Rebellion. Following the execution, there had been an enormous hue and cry in Ontario, which precipitated Wolseley's troops moving west. Concerned for his safety, Riel fled Manitoba when Wolseley arrived and sought sanctuary in the Dakotas.

Donald A. Smith, a Hudson's Bay Company representative in Canada and a government agent, was asked to act as the temporary governor, until the arrival of the lieutenant governor. This established a new civilian authority in the province.

Adams Archibald, who had spoken so eloquently in the House of Commons on the Manitoba Act, arrived as the newly appointed lieutenant governor. He moved quickly to establish his governor's council, assigning Marc-Amable Girard as provincial treasurer, and Alfred Boyd, a merchant and trader who had immigrated from England, as provincial secretary. The latter prominent post, similar to the former Secretary of State for Canada, included responsibilities for elections, formal documents and records, administration of the civil service, as well as miscellaneous government duties. As the senior executive councillor, Boyd has been considered by some to be Manitoba's first premier, although it is interesting to note that in Room 254 in the Manitoba Legislature, the room with the portraits of the early premiers of Manitoba, there are no paintings of either Boyd or Riel.

Boyd's new executive council recruited a small police force, commissioned magistrates, proceeded to take a census, and set up constituencies in preparation for an election in December. The same parish lines used for the selection of representatives for Riel's provisional government were employed. Twelve members representing predominantly French-speaking parishes, and twelve representing predominantly English-speaking parishes were elected. Seventeen of the twenty-four members of the legislature were sympathetic to the former provisional government, demonstrating the high level of continuity between the newly constituted authority and Riel's caretaker authority.

In early December 1870, dogged by criticism from his constituents who were asking for more jails and bridges, and for supporting public works in the new community of St. Boniface, Boyd resigned from his position as provincial secretary.

Marc Girard became the next senior member of the executive council and is often considered to be Manitoba's second premier, serving until March 14, 1871. (Girard does have a portrait in the legislature as premier, but it recognizes not this first term, but his second term in 1874.) Born and educated in Québec, he was a protégé of George Etienne Cartier, who had arrived in Manitoba in 1870 with Archibishop Taché to help ensure a strong francophone presence in the new government. He was elected in the riding of St. Boniface and would later serve for a period as premier in 1874, and then afterwards in John Norquay's provincial cabinet from 1879 to 1883.

In January 1871, Lieutenant Governor Archibald added three new members to the executive council. Thomas Howard was appointed as provincial secretary and James McKay was included as member without portfolio. Henry Joseph (Hynes) Clarke, a journalist and established criminal lawyer, became attorney general and the senior minister. As leading minister in the cabinet, he is often considered Manitoba's third premier, serving until July 8, 1874. Clarke is the first leader to have a painting recognizing his premiership hanging in the present Manitoba Legislature.

The first of a long line of Masons to serve as premier of the province, Clarke had moved with his family from his native Ireland to Canada when he was three years old. After a successful career as a lawyer in Montréal, he relocated to Manitoba in 1870, to assist Adams Archibald in the establishment of a provincial government.

The new session of the legislature began on March 14, 1871. It met in the home of Mr. A.G.B. Bannatyne, one of Winnipeg's wealthiest and most influential citizens. The members sat for six weeks and passed forty-three bills. The government established a system of courts based on the British model of English common law and created statute law which followed that of Ontario. As in Québec, separate school systems were provided for French Catholics and English Protestants.

Clarke's relationship with Adams Archibald was turbulent due to disagreements on policy, but under his administration surveys of lands within the province were completed, and in August 1871, Treaties One and Two were signed with First Nations representatives in Manitoba. Treaty One (with the Cree), signed on August 3rd, provided for the surrender of lands included in the new province, and some areas to the west, in exchange for some short-term and long-term benefits. Treaty Two (with the "Chippewa" or Ojibwe), which covered the area near the southern parts of Lake Winnipeg, around most of Lake Manitoba and west to the Saskatchewan border, followed three weeks later. Treaties Three to Five (encompassing most of the remainder of what is now Manitoba) followed between 1873 and 1875. In November 1873, the City of Winnipeg was formally established by an act of the legislature.

Adams Archibald was replaced as lieutenant governor by Alexander Morris in 1873. Clarke's administration lost a vote of confidence in early 1874, and Girard became premier for several months until the fall of that year, when he was forced to resign because of simmering ethnic tensions. Richard Atkinson Davis, one of Girard's ministers, was asked to form a new government.

Davis faced difficult fiscal realities. Though the province was paid a subsidy from the Government of Canada, he claimed it was "not enough to pay the expenses of running a respectable seaside hotel." [4] He was successful in ensuring that the route of the transcontinental rail line went through Winnipeg and not Selkirk, but for the most part, his term as premier was marked by cutbacks in spending, including the abolition of the unelected Upper House (the provincial equivalent of the Canadian Senate).

Davis resigned as premier in 1878, paving the way for the leadership of John Norquay, an Orcadian mixed-blood native of St. Andrew's, Manitoba. Norquay, who with the help of his mentor, Bishop David Anderson, had learned French, Latin and Greek, had begun a career in teaching. In 1870, he was elected to the Manitoba Legislature representing High Bluff and was appointed to the executive council (or cabinet) a year later.

---

[4] Adam Shortt and Arthur Doughty (eds): *Canada and Its Provinces, Vol XIX, The Prairie Provinces*, (Edinburgh University Press, 1914) p. 107.

During Norquay's tenure, the boundaries of Manitoba were extended in 1881, westward to the present boundary and north to the 52nd parallel. To the east, there was an extended court battle over Rat Portage (now Kenora), but the muscle of the larger province of Ontario and the Privy Council ruling of 1874 finally resolved this issue in Ontario's favour, settling the provincial boundary where it stands today.

Norquay wanted to reduce high transportation costs by further developing rail lines in Manitoba. The Canadian Pacific Railway line was completed in November 1885, providing a trans-continental link, but the demand for additional railway connections for farm communities was substantial. His legislation to permit construction of a Red River Valley railway in order to end the CPR monopoly was disallowed by Ottawa. When his government ignored Ottawa and issued $300,000 in Manitoba bonds to finance construction, Prime Minister John A. Macdonald refused to make the land transfer that was to be the security on the bonds. In an impossible situation, Norquay resigned on December 22, 1887.

He was replaced by a Minnedosa farmer, physician and politician, Dr. D.H. Harrison. When Harrison's choice for provincial secretary, Joseph Burke, was defeated in an election in St. Francois Xavier, he, too, was forced to resign, ending a string of non-partisan provincial leaders and paving the way for Manitoba's first Liberal premier, Thomas Greenway.

Above, Manitoba's first Liberal premier, Thomas Greenway, c. 1890 and right, perhaps the most powerful provincial and federal minister of the era, Clifford Sifton, c. 1898

Archives of Manitoba N–14998

Archives of Manitoba N–199/1

3

The Siren Call
1888–1908

Thomas Greenway and Clifford Sifton

*"He was for a quarter of a century the staunch friend of
the west and never wavered in his confidence in the great
future before this part of Canada ... No man has left a
more lasting impression on Manitoba than has Hon
Thomas Greenway."*
—Thomas J. Johnson
in the *Manitoba Free Press*

Manitoba was just eighteen years old when the Liberals, led
by Thomas Greenway, swept into power in the July 1888 election,
capturing thirty-three of the province's thirty-eight seats. The like-
able, down-to-earth farmer and merchant from Crystal City was
both a visionary and a man of dogged tenacity. He had turned to
politics to effect change in the province, especially in the area of
agriculture and his new government got down to business quickly,
delivering a throne speech in August.

The first speaker, chosen for the honour by the new premier,
was twenty-seven-year old Clifford Sifton. The lawyer and newly
elected MLA for Brandon was well-turned out, with an elegant
moustache and attractive wave in his hair. But behind the charming
good looks and distinguished demeanour was a man of action with a
passion for the prairies. His address emphasized the government's
vision of increased immigration to Manitoba, improved education,
and competition with the railways to enhance railway access and
lower freight rates. It was a singular sign of promise to come.

Over the next two decades, Sifton and Greenway would have

a major impact on the development of Manitoba, spearheading the immigration of large numbers of people from the United States and Europe, particularly from England, Poland, Ukraine and Russia. Later, as federal minister of the Interior and lead federal minister for Manitoba, Sifton would continue to work closely with Premier Greenway, always pushing for immigrant settlers on the western prairies.

Watching his protégé from his seat in the middle of the front bench, Thomas Greenway no doubt smiled with pleasure, pondering the previous nine years in the legislature that had brought him to this point. Many early Liberals played a role in the development and strength of the provincial Liberal Party, but under Greenway's leadership, the Liberals had earned the right to govern the province.

The story of the rise to power of the first Liberal government in Manitoba properly begins soon after the birth of Manitoba in 1870, when fledgling allegiances were forged among like-minded individuals who had thrown their hats into the political ring. While some early premiers, including John Norquay, tried to operate less partisan governments, many legislators had clearly declared their party alliance.

The first identifiable Liberal MLA was Edward Henry George Gunson Hay, (E.H.G.G. Hay) or "Alphabetical Hay", as he was known locally.[1] A miller in St. Andrews who built one of the West's first gristmills, Hay was elected a member of the first Manitoba legislature in December 1870. He had come to North America as a cabin boy of thirteen, learning his trade as a machinist with steamship entrepreneur J. J. Hill in St. Paul, Minnesota. He arrived at the Red River colony in 1864 and later taught night school and served as a lieutenant in the 1st Lisgar Rifles. He represented St. Andrews South in the Manitoba Legislature until 1874 and later St. Clements in 1879, and distinguished himself as leader of Her Majesty's Opposition.

---

[1] J.M. Bumstead, *Dictionary of Manitoba Biography*, (Winnipeg: University of Manitoba Press, 1999), p. 107. In about 1881, Hay moved to Portage la Prairie. There he opened a foundry that remained in operation until 1893. In 1889 he was appointed police magistrate and was made clerk of the works at St. Andrews Lock in 1900. He retired in 1911 and died at Lockport in 1918. "Alphabetical" Hay acquired the Firth house near Lockport and served as Clerk of the Works during the building of the Locks. He was generous to a fault. Hay lived like a country squire; he lent or gave money to hapless neighbours. When he died in 1919, there was precious little left. Helen Harriet, the middle daughter of E.H.G.G. Hay and his wife, Elizabeth Gibson Hay, was born in 1870. For many years she ran a teahouse and was a noted entrepreneur in the Lockport area. (From: Armstrong, Colleen (editor) *Extraordinary Ordinary Women The Manitoba Clubs of the Canadian Federation of University Women*, Winnipeg, 2000.)

Another early Liberal was journalist Robert Cunningham who had come west in 1869 as a special correspondent for the *Toronto Globe* and the *Toronto Telegram* to cover the story of the provisional government under Louis Riel.[2] Though expelled by Riel shortly after his arrival, he returned in 1870 to begin *The Manitoban* with William Coldwell. Gradually, he developed a friendship with Riel and came to appreciate his work in advancing the rights of the Métis people. In 1872, now supported by Riel, Cunningham was elected the member of Parliament (MP) for Marquette. In Ottawa, where he spoke consistently on behalf of the Métis community, Cunningham became an example of the early links between Liberals and the Métis people. He also supported the settlement of Manitoba land claims and a general amnesty for those, like Louis Riel, who were involved in the provisional government and the execution of Thomas Scott. Cunningham was re-elected in 1874 but died later that year on his return to Manitoba.

In the second provincial election, in 1874, Alphonse Fortunat Martin, a surveyor and civil engineer, was elected Liberal MLA for Ste. Agathe. He served as opposition leader in the legislature from 1875 until his defeat in 1879. After an unsuccessful attempt to again secure a seat in 1883, he was elected MLA for Morris in 1886. Martin supported Manitoba First, and its demands for provincial rights; the extension of the Manitoba boundary to Hudson Bay, and the province's separate school system.[3]

Like Alphonse Martin, William Fisher Luxton joined the legislature in 1874, as the Liberal MLA for Rockwood. An outspoken and fearless journalist who began the Liberal newspaper, the *Manitoba Free Press,* in 1872, Luxton went on to become the MP for South Winnipeg from 1886 to 1888. He returned to provincial politics in 1888 and was present on the front bench when Greenway became premier.[4]

Robert Watson, elected to the House of Commons as a Liberal in 1882 and 1887, was the only Liberal MP from west of the Lakehead in those parliaments. Born in Elora, Ontario, to Scottish parents, he

---

[2] Cunningham was born in Ayrshire, Scotland in 1836. He was educated at Glasgow College and the University of London before coming to Canada in 1868.

[3] A. F. Martin was born in Rimouski and educated at Rimouski College, where he later studied surveying and civil engineering. He became a Dominion land surveyor in 1871 and came to Manitoba the following year, to settle in West Lynn. Employed in various surveys, he authored *Martin on Practical Surveys*, which was published in 1883.

[4] Luxton's political goals were prohibition, a purely secular school system, abolition of French as an official language, and the demise of the CPR.

became a millwright and moved to Manitoba in 1876. He was re-elected as an MP in 1891, but resigned to become minister of Public Works in the Greenway government. He continued to serve as MLA in 1892 and 1896, but was defeated in 1900, the year he was called to the Senate.

John Wright Sifton, father of Clifford Sifton, served as Liberal MLA for St. Clements from 1878 to 1879. He became speaker for a brief period in 1879 and went on to become the MP for Brandon from 1881–1883.[5] During this period, J.W. Sifton worked closely with Greenway to oppose Prime Minister John A. Macdonald's disallowance of several railway bills passed in the Manitoba Legislature. The bills would have permitted the establishment of a railway in direct competition with the Canadian Pacific Railway.

Thomas Greenway came to Manitoba in the fall of 1878 to scout potential locations for settlers.[6] He was attracted to a region of southern Manitoba near where the Pembina River expanded to form Rock Lake. The lake provided good fishing and the open mixed grass prairie was prime potential farmland, ready to be developed for agricultural purposes.

One of the best descriptions of the region is from a report of the Palliser expedition of 1857–1860. Palliser had come from the north and passed through the Pembina Valley before reaching a cone-shaped hill, called "pilot mound".[7] This mound, very close to today's community of Pilot Mound, and just a few miles north of where Greenway would settle at Crystal City, was an indigenous tribal burial mound and probably also a sacred and ceremonial place that served as a guide or pilot to early travellers. Artifacts found there, with origins as far away as Lake Superior to the east and Mexico to the south, suggest it had been a landmark and gathering place for millennia. It is likely that when Greenway arrived less than two decades later, the local region looked quite similar.

Approaching the "cone-shaped Hill of the Great Medicine

---

[5] J.M. Bumstead, *Dictionary of Manitoba Biography*, p. 227. John Wright Sifton was "Born in Middlesex Country, Upper Canada", of Irish origins. He moved to Selkirk, Manitoba, in 1875 and became a successful contractor, mainly involved with railways and telegraph construction. After spending several years in California in the 1880s, he returned to become vice-president of the company that owned the *Manitoba Free Press* in 1902 and subsequently its president. Sifton was also an active temperance advocate.

[6] Keith Wilson, *Thomas Greenway*, (Winnipeg: Faculty of Education, University of Manitoba, 1985), p. 11.

[7] Penny Ham, *Place Names of Manitoba*, (Saskatoon: Western Producer Prairie Books, 1980), p. 101.

Dance, Paquewin" from the northeast, they travelled into the Pembina Valley along a "fair, winding road" which went down the "steep, wooded" side of the valley and up the other side toward today's Pilot Mound. As was noted, "This valley marked the edge of *la grande prairie.* To the east, the country was wooded and irregular; to the west [toward Pilot Mound], at the higher level, there was nothing but bare prairie lands." [8]

Greenway was attracted to a spot just south of the pilot mound at the junction of the Boundary Trail and Crystal Creek. There, in the shelter of the creek bank, his group camped for the night. "[S]askatoon, cranberry, chokecherry and wild plums grew in abundance." In addition, there were "wild fowl in great number … herds of white-tailed deer, [and] The waters of the creek were teeming with fish ..."

As he sat by the campfire, he dreamed that he would "build a great city, which would become the capital of Manitoba. It was to be a prairie city, a garden city, such as the world had not yet seen. Here, on the banks of Crystal Creek, his dream intensified, and he felt this was the place to begin." [9]

Greenway was a strapping man with a broad forehead and shoulders, and a personality to match. He had come to Upper Canada with his parents, Thomas and Elizabeth, when he was six years old and the family eventually pioneered on land in Huron County. With the death of his father in 1849, eleven-year old Thomas had to assume much of the responsibility for the family. He worked as a store clerk and eventually set up his own business as a general merchant in Devon (later Centralia). In January 1860, he married Annie Hicks of Devon and together they had seven children. In the ensuing years, Greenway's business prospered and he opened additional stores in Crediton and Exeter.

Popular as well as industrious, he was elected reeve of Stephen Township at age twenty-nine, and held that office until 1874. Running as a Conservative, he unsuccessfully contested three federal and provincial elections in the early 1870s. During his seven years as reeve, Greenway grew progressively interested in issues surrounding settlement and the role and development of the railways across Canada. He knew his own business suffered because

---

[8]   Irene M. Spry, *The Palliser Expedition: The Dramatic Story of Western Canadian Exploration 1857–1860,* (Toronto: The Macmillan Co. of Canada, 1963), pp. 46–47.

[9]   Susan Hiebert, *Thomas Greenway: the farmer-premier* (Crystal City Community Printing Museum Inc., 1994) p. 6–7.

of protective tariffs on manufactured goods, which raised prices and decreased sales.[10] In 1875, when he was elected as the federal MP for the riding of South Huron, he became immersed in the divide between the Macdonald Conservatives with their National Policy of high tariffs, and Alexander Mackenzie's Liberals, who supported free trade. It was this growing opposition to the tariffs, that prompted Greenway to switch his allegiance to the Liberal Party.

He emerged from his years as a Liberal MP a strong supporter of free trade, as well as a politician concerned with the settlement and growth of Canada and the role of the railways. He had increased his understanding of the country as a whole through discussions with elected members from across Canada and had learned, in detail, the status of the plans for railways to the West. He had likely read Sir William Francis Butler's *The Great Lone Land*, and he had probably heard of John Palliser's report of the arid lands in Western Canada.

Most important, however, was the meeting he had with John Macoun, the professor and naturalist who had travelled west in 1872 and 1875. Macoun lectured widely throughout Ontario following his expeditions, but in contrast to Palliser, Macoun was convinced that "the so-called arid country was one of unsurpassed fertility and that it was literally the Garden of the whole country." [11] Macoun's enthusiasm for the fertility of Western Canada was infectious and Greenway, inspired by the possibilities, became an evangelist in spreading Macoun's word about Manitoba's potential.

Greenway, along with his brother William and six colleagues, set out to organize the Rock Lake Colonization Company. The politician and entrepreneur travelled extensively in his part of Ontario, painting a picture of Manitoba and its opportunities for "the poor and struggling man ... the richness of the virgin soil, the almost limitless expanse of the area now occupied only by feathered songsters or trodden by the untamed buffalo or waked by the echoes of the prairie dog's howl." [12] He found willing listeners in Centralia who, disheartened by second-rate agricultural land and the back-breaking work of clearing forest, were still looking for Eden.

Greenway's timing was auspicious. There was much excitement

---

[10] Wilson, *Thomas Greenway*, p. 11.

[11] John Macoun, *Autobiography of John Macoun, Canadian Explorer and Naturalist, 1831–1920*, (Ottawa Field-Naturalist's Club, originally published in 1922, republished 1979) p. 153.

[12] Wilson, *Thomas Greenway*, p. 11.

about Manitoba and the CPR was soon to make train travel possible to Winnipeg and westward. Just two years before, in 1876, the first exports of Red Fife—the hard kernelled wheat with a high gluten content in demand by British millers—had left Manitoba for England. The words of John Macoun rang loud: "there is actually no limit, but the want of a market, to the wheat crop of the North-West." [13]

The promise of Manitoba was amplified by publications like Macoun's 1877 report, which described the wonderful prairie land that did not need to be cleared of forests before it could be farmed. For many, the opportunity was too good to refuse, and in the spring and early summer of 1879, Greenway brought three groups of settlers to the region just east of Rock Lake along Crystal Creek and established Crystal City. On March 27, 1879, *The Exeter Times* reported on the departure of the first eager group of settlers. [14]

Arrangements were made to start on the 25th of the month for Rock Lake region, about 18 miles north of the International boundary, and a brisk trade has been done by the merchants in the vicinity of the lines of goods, which would be most needed in the 'great lone land.' On Tuesday last quite a number of wagons, laden with bedding, pots, pans, kettles, with here and there a stray article of household furniture, passed through Exeter on the way to Centralia. An immense crowd, numbering several hundred, flocked to the little village from all parts of the neighbouring country to see the voyageurs off and shower their good wishes upon them. Very few women went with the party, it being deemed advisable to leave the gentler sex behind in comfortable homes until some preparations have been made to receive them properly in their far-off future homes. At Centralia, the Greenway party was joined by a large party from Listowel, Lucknow, Wingham and other places up north, and shortly after nine o'clock the huge train, numbering 21 cars, freight and passengers, under charge of Conductor Brown steamed out of the station yard amid the intense enthusiasm of the

---

[13] Grant MacEwan, *Between the Red and the Rockies*, (Western Producer Prairie Books, Saskatoon) p. 43.

[14] Wilson, *Thomas Greenway*, p. 11.

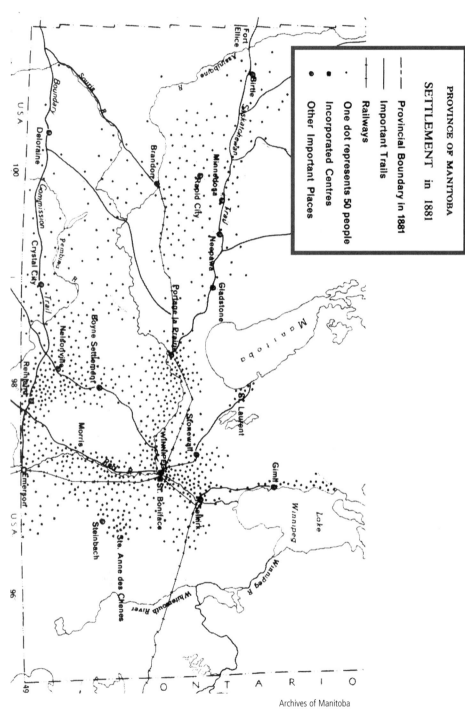

PROVINCE OF MANITOBA
SETTLEMENT in 1881

- - - Provincial Boundary in 1881
——— Important Trails
Railways
● One dot represents 50 people
■ Incorporated Centres
• Other Important Places

Archives of Manitoba

assembled multitude, who crowded the platform and
grounds adjacent, waving handkerchiefs, shouting
huzzas, and bidding a fond good-bye to those who
were going on the long and toilsome journey to
make their homes where the sun declines.

The town of Crystal City was established on Greenway's half
section of land—initially one tent for the dormitory and one tent
for the kitchen and dining room.

His settlers were only a small part of the estimated 11,500 new
arrivals in Manitoba in 1879, just a few hundred less than the entire
population of the postage stamp province at the time of its birth.
Thousands more poured in over the next two years and by 1881,
the census numbers swelled to 65,954.

As more settlers arrived, Greenway focused his efforts on
improving their circumstances and returned to politics—as the
elected member of the Legislative Assembly (MLA) for the newly
formed provincial constituency of Mountain. He continued to
emphasize the themes that had long been important to him:
farming and increasing and improving settlement. Believing competition was best for railway development and for reducing transportation costs, he advocated increasing railway lines and moving
away from Macdonald's national protective tariff policy.

His opposition to the monopoly of the CPR hit close to home
in 1879, when the Manitoba South Western Colonization Railway
received a provincial charter to build a line from Winnipeg to the
southwest. Greenway hoped and expected that the line would con-
nect to Crystal City, which had been designated the county town
for Rock Lake County.

In 1882 however, the federal government disallowed the
provincial railway charter, citing that it violated the CPR's rights
to a monopoly on all railway construction in the West for a period
of twenty years. Greenway spoke out forcefully and publicly to
denounce the federal government's stand against provincial legislation, and as a result, emerged as the leader of the Opposition in
the Manitoba Legislature. Greenway and others who supported
him, like John Sifton, "touched a responsive chord in the population. Provincial rights agitation spread like a prairie fire." [15] The
opposition united under the banner of the Provincial Rights Party,
promoting Greenway's broader agenda of improved provincial

---

[15] D.J. Hall, *Clifford Sifton: Volume 1: The Young Napoleon 1861-1900*, (University of British
Columbia Press, Vancouver, 1981) p. 20.

control of public lands and settlement and growth.

In mid-1883, the railway line to southwestern Manitoba—still firmly under the control of the CPR—reached Manitou and appeared to be heading for Crystal City. Optimism was in the air. The town had sprouted three general stores, two hardware stores, a drug store, a furniture store, a blacksmith's shop, two hotels, a flour-mill and a Methodist Church. Greenway had brought in a printing press and launched *The Rock Lake Herald*. His personal empire was growing, too. He had built his own home and landscaped the yard with trees and shrubs, laid out a garden and began developing the Prairie Home Stock Farm to grow wheat and raise purebred cattle. His second wife, Emma (Essary), whom he had married in 1877 after the death of Annie Devon, and the seven children of his first marriage plus two new arrivals, had all come with him to Manitoba. In the next few years, Thomas and Emma Greenway would have five more children, bringing the total to fourteen.

The future needed the railway, but the CPR made a decision that further intensified Greenway's determination to end its monopoly as soon as possible. The tracks were laid a mile and a half north of Crystal City, forcing the townsite to move in order to prosper.

Greenway had become opposition leader after the provincial election of 1883, and throughout the decade continued to build the Liberal Party in Manitoba, including in its ranks established Liberals as well as members of the former Provincial Rights Party.

In 1885 and 1886, vigorous efforts were made to create local Liberal organizations across the province, and conventions were held each year to build the party's presence and platform. At the second party convention in 1886, Greenway had to beat back a challenge to his leadership. He enlarged his vision and the scope of his opposition to the Conservative government of John Norquay and was vocal on various matters—including improving democracy by moving to a one man, one vote system. At the time, only men who owned property or who were tenants rated on the assessment roll could vote. But a person could vote in as many electoral divisions as desired as long as he fulfilled one of these conditions in each division. The result was "that in almost the majority of elections the outside vote corruptly brought in decided the results of the election." [16]

Greenway also argued for improving the function of the legislature. "The house should have been called together at the proper time of the year," said Greenway in 1885; "other provinces have

---

[16] Record of the Greenway Government 1888–1892. Document in the Manitoba Archives.

Archives of Manitoba Drawn for Thomas Greenway c. 1900

PRAIRIE HOME STOCK FARM

fixed times for the sessions and have run a lot smoother." [17]

He was a powerful orator, as witnessed in a speech on April 22, 1885; his only speech in which the full text has been saved. Greenway began slowly, using his voice and his words as tools to build his point—that the premier, John Norquay, had lost his sense of direction, and had been advocating for the Dominion government rather than for the best interests of Manitoba.

> A year ago, on the 16th of April, the hon gentleman [Premier Norquay] stood in this legislature and advocated the interests of the Province of Manitoba. A week ago last night, I think it was, the hon gentleman stood up, and having taken a brief on the other side, undertook to advocate the claims of the Dominion of

---

[17] From the newspaper reports of the day as recorded in the *Hansard* documents in the library of the Legislature of Manitoba.

Canada as against those of the Province of Manitoba.
I am not judging the hon gentleman too harshly
because I have it out of his own mouth. He says, 'Do
you propose to bind me by what I said last year in
the little pamphlet which was circulated throughout
the length and breadth of Manitoba? You should not
do so; that speech was made as a lawyer would make
it, for the purpose of making out a case.' [18]

And here, Greenway took hold. Norquay had clearly said—
don't believe what I said, I was only making a case. Time and again
Greenway returned to this theme—that the premier himself had
said he was not to be taken seriously.

I am forgetting the hon. Gentleman was only making
a case—he did not mean it ...

Manitoba's premier had come back from Ottawa with a deal
that was not good enough—a deal that fell short of what he had
said he was going to obtain. Greenway pointed out that Norquay
should have followed his true calling and been a lawyer making a
case—rather than a premier whom people expected to be able to
trust. He further tore into Norquay, mocking his position: "the idea
of confining a gentleman of the transcendent abilities of the premier
of the Province to the banner fields of facts is altogether absurd."
    Greenway concluded that the settlement with the national
government was so appalling that Norquay, in his new capacity
as lawyer, must have gone over to the other side—and was now
trying to make a case for the national government:

I submit it is a pity that any influence could have
been brought to bear, and that anything any body of
men could offer, could have induced a gentleman of his
ability to take a retainer on the other side, which he
has evidently done.

When he finished, there was loud and prolonged applause.
Greenway had made his own case well: Manitoba needed a premier
who meant what he said, a premier who would argue for the

---

[18] Thomas Greenway – Speech on the Estimates delivered by Thomas Greenway MPP in the Manitoba Legislature, April 22nd, 1885. *Winnipeg Free Press* print – P 3402 f.6 in the Archives of Manitoba).

province, not one who would take the side of the Dominion government.

Manitobans now knew clearly that Greenway was on their side, and cracks that had begun during Norquay's leadership now threatened to crumble his foundation of support.

During the 1880s, Norquay promised to build a railway in the Red River Valley and to start a new line to Hudson Bay. In 1887, he issued $300,000 in Manitoba bonds, secured by a grant of land to be provided by Ottawa. Prime Minister John A. Macdonald did not transfer the land, resulting in the provincial government issuing bonds without collateral. It was a financial and public relations disaster and led to Norquay's resignation. He was replaced as premier by D.H. Harrison of Minnedosa who, unable to gain the support of the majority of MLAs, was forced to resign on January 13, 1888. Three days later Lieutenant Governor James Cox Aikins called on Thomas Greenway to form a government.

Greenway and his caucus moved quickly to improve the democratic process in Manitoba by passing legislation providing for a man (at the time only men voted) to have only one vote instead of being able to vote in every constituency in which the person held property. This much fairer system was implemented in time for the election of July 1888.

He then addressed the railway situation, adjourning the legislature to travel to Ottawa to negotiate a better deal for Manitoba and end the CPR monopoly. When Ottawa held back in granting concessions, Greenway "bluntly threatened to break off all negotiations." [19]

His threats were effective. When he returned to Manitoba six weeks later, the monopoly of the CPR had ended and John A. Macdonald agreed not to disallow further provincial chartering of railways. Greenway's next decision was to complete the Red River Valley Railway in a contract signed with the Northern Pacific, but before the railway could be completed there was a battle at Fort Whyte, where the new railway was to cross the CPR line. William Whyte, the CPR's western superintendent, was determined to block the advance of the new railway toward Portage la Prairie. He had a locomotive ditched across the path of the oncoming railway tracks and defended the site with 200 men ready to fight. As the two sides faced off, 'Fighting Joe Martin', Greenway's attorney general, took public opposition to a fevered pitch and the legal fight all the way

---

[19] Press clippings in the Manitoba Legislature files, including those from Winnipeg and Ottawa at the time of Greenway's death.

to the justices at the Supreme Court, who ruled that the crossing could proceed.

In his election campaign that summer, Greenway promised to establish provincial lines that would continue to reduce freight rates. He further proposed to improve the province's financial position, to boost immigration, improve democracy by the move to one man one vote, and to develop the province's educational system.[20]

THEY ARE ALL VERY SORROWFUL AT THE FUNERAL.

Archives of Manitoba, Transportation-Railway-1888

Greenway successfully ended the CPR monopoly and brought competition to Manitoba. Here he drives the carriage while Sir John A. Macdonald, Donald A. Smith, Charles Tupper, George Stephen and Cornelius Van Horne walk mournfully beside.

Once elected, his first task was to reduce the cost of government and to put the province's finances in order. The Norquay government had left a debt of about $1.6 million. In its last year in power, the cost of the civil service and its supporting infrastructure was just under $258,000. Greenway decreased the cost by about forty per cent in each of the next three years, largely by eliminating unnecessary expenditures in various departments and by reductions in areas like printing, advertising and stationery. As reported later: "a special law was passed to regulate public printing and thus put an end to scandalous waste, and retrenchment was effected in every department."[21]

---

[20] Record of the Greenway Government 1888-1892. Document in the Archives of Manitoba.

[21] Press clippings in the Manitoba legislature files, including those from Winnipeg and Ottawa at the time of Greenway's death.

The savings resulted in improving the efficiency of government and allowed increased expenditures in critical areas like education, health, public works, immigration, agriculture and drainage.

Greenway's actions in support of farmers and his alliance with farm groups galvanized agriculture as a vital force in Manitoba politics. At first, he was his own minister of Agriculture but later chose his close friend Valentine Winkler to serve in this portfolio. Winkler—for whom the present City of Winkler is named—arrived in Manitoba in 1879, took up a homestead in the Morden area and became the first reeve of the municipality of Stanley. When the railway was completed and Valentine Winkler was elected to the provincial legislature in 1892, he and Greenway frequently travelled together by train between Morden and Winnipeg. During Winkler's term in cabinet, legislation was introduced to enable settlers in the Interlake area to obtain cattle on credit; individuals selling farm produce were required to be bonded and licenced; the sale of farm machinery was regulated and a Provincial Weeds Commission was appointed.

Greenway himself "was thoroughly conversant with everything affecting the farmer." Even Rodmond Roblin, who led the Conservative Party after Hugh John Macdonald, conceded "Few men understood the needs of the western farmer better than Hon. Thos Greenway and this fact was generally known."[22]

As a leader in his community, he held annual fairs at the Prairie Home Farm, encouraging farmers to raise the very best produce. His own farm became a model and one of the best in the West. In his last term of office particularly, Greenway worked diligently to promote drainage efforts to improve agricultural yields and to decrease risks to farmers. By 1901, there were 2,756,106 acres under crop in Manitoba.

> [Greenway] ...took a lively interest in everything that could enhance the value of land and promote the agricultural development of the province. It was on this ground that he went into the fight for railway competition with such determination, that he advocated a vigorous immigration policy, that he gave generous support to disseminate scientific knowledge among the farmers, and that he planned for reclamation of the swamp lands. In 1893, he did not hesitate

---

[22] Press clippings in the Manitoba Legislature files, including those from Winnipeg and Ottawa at the time of Greenway's death.

to assume large responsibilities to place Manitoba property before the public at the Chicago World's Fair, when the Dominion government shirked its duty. [23]

The breaking of the railway monopoly was proclaimed a major victory for farmers who now had a competitive option to export their grain, and throughout Greenway's tenure as premier the expansion of railways continued. Typical was the 100 miles of railway completed to Dauphin in 1896.[24] Enthusiasm was high and some of the new settlers pitched in to help build the railway, rather like the way many neighbours gathered together for a barn-raising bee to put up a barn for a new arrival. In return, the new railway, (now named Canadian Northern Railway,) provided free seed wheat in the Dauphin area in the spring of 1897. The masterminds behind this stretch of track included William Mackenzie, the financing guru, and Donald Mann, the practical construction genius. They went on to complete the CNR as a transcontinental competitor to the CPR. What began as a small line to Dauphin thus became a national railway. Manitoba, and entrepreneurs starting in Manitoba, were becoming a national force.

In 1897, Clifford Sifton, Greenway's former colleague and now a minister in the federal government, completed the negotiations for the historic Crow's Nest Pass freight rates. In this agreement, the government subsidized construction of the CPR line going through the Crow's Nest Pass from Lethbridge, Alberta to Nelson, British Columbia. In return, the CPR

> agreed to a subsidy of $11,000 per mile, up to $3,630,000, for the line [to be constructed] between Lethbridge and Nelson [through the Crow's Nest Pass]. In return the CPR agreed to reduce rates by one-third on green and fresh fruits, by one-fifth on coal oil, and by one-tenth on a series of consumer goods vital to the farmer: cordage, binder twine, agricultural implements, iron, wire, glass, roofing and construction paper, construction felt, paints and oils, livestock, woodenware and household furniture.

---

[23] Press clippings in the Manitoba Legislature files, including those from Winnipeg and Ottawa at the time of Greenway's death.

[24] Margaret McWilliams, *Manitoba Milestones*, (Toronto: J.M. Dent and Sons Ltd., 1928), pp. 173–174.

A reduction of 3 cents per hundred pounds on flour and grain freight rates from points in the North-West to Fort William was accepted. [25]

Not only were the reductions agreed to, but the agreement also specified "no higher rates than such reduced rates or tolls shall be hereafter charged by the Company … between the points afore-said." This clause would keep grain freight rates low for almost a century.

Archives of Manitoba

The interior of Winnipeg's Immigration Hall in April 1893. By the late 1890s, the tide of immigrants threatened to flood Manitoba's facilities as Greenway and Sifton combined to vigorously promote Western Canadian settlement.

During his first term of office Greenway almost doubled funding for education and substantially increased the grant to the University of Manitoba. In 1886-87 the provincial funding for education was $66,000. By 1891, Greenway had increased it to $120,000 and by 1900 to $321,240. He had often debated the possibilities of a public school system with teachers and friends at Crystal Creek and his platform in 1888 emphasized his aim, "to develop the educational system and to increase facilities for education, to increase the grant for school purposes so as to lessen school taxation." He established a Public School System in the province as well as a full Department

---

[25] Hall, Ibid., pp. 154–155.

of Education with a mandate for providing a non-denominational curriculum. By 1900, education was the largest single area of funding in the Greenway administration.

The extent to which education should occur in languages other than English in Manitoba schools, and the extent to which there should be religious education in schools, were major and emotional issues during Greenway's premiership. It was over these issues that Manitoba became "the storm centre of politics in the Dominion." [26] The education system for Manitoba was originally to have separate publicly funded Catholic and Protestant school systems. Changing from this approach caused great controversy.

In the end, the Laurier-Greenway compromise of 1897 provided for one public school system, but with a level of balance when it came to the language of instruction. For example, bilingual French and English education was provided for "when ten pupils in any school speak the French language." [27] Similar opportunity was provided for other linguistic groups where there was a minimum of ten students who spoke another language.

Health care also received greater attention under Greenway's administration. In a decade, he increased the annual health care budget almost twenty-four fold, from $10,899 just before he was elected, to $240,670 in 1898. He improved funding for hospitals and founded the Institute for the Deaf, the first of its kind on the Canadian prairies.

By providing a climate for growth and expansion, and by operating a more efficient government, Greenway created the conditions for increased provincial revenues and increased investments in the province's public and social infrastructure.

However, Greenway and his government fell short when it came to protecting the constitutional rights of French-speaking Manitobans. In his first term as premier, Greenway's government became embroiled in what has been referred to as a "prairie fire"— a growing firestorm of public sentiment pushing for English as the provincial language and repudiating the use of French in the legislature and in the business of the legislature. This was totally contrary to the Manitoba Act of 1870, and remains a black mark on Greenway's record. The initiative was led by two members of cabinet, James

---

[26] Press clippings in the Manitoba Legislature files, including those from Winnipeg and Ottawa at the time of Greenway's death.

[27] James A. Jackson, *The Centennial History of Manitoba*, (McClelland and Stewart Ltd., Toronto, 1970) pp. 149-150.

Smart, the public works minister, and Joseph Martin, the attorney general. Joseph Martin was caught in an August 1889 Portage la Prairie meeting where D'Alton McCarthy spoke in inflammatory language against the need for the use of French in Manitoba. Though Martin was privately and publicly repudiated by Greenway, a public outcry was launched. It led, in 1890, to the passage of a bill that made English the official language of Manitoba and ended the use of French in the legislature, as well as its bills, its reports and its journals. It was a most regrettable point in Manitoba history, and it was not corrected until after the courts overturned the bill in 1979.

Greenway continued to play a major role in promoting immigration to Manitoba, which had a population of about 120,000 when he became premier. This number grew to just over 150,000 by 1891, and to 255,000 in 1901. Greenway took on the portfolio of immigration minister and set up provincial offices in Toronto, Moncton and Liverpool.

> Greenway took an immense amount of trouble visiting in person all the principal agricultural districts of England and Scotland and entering into relations with the tenant farmers and agricultural landowners. His efforts were very successful. It was reported that the body of emigrants to Manitoba taken by the Allan steamer, 'Parisan' is said to be one of the finest that has ever gone from this country. [28]

Manitoba had already opened its arms to newcomers from 1873–1878, when the federal Liberal government in Ottawa made arrangements for Icelandic and Mennonite settlers to come to the province. New Iceland was established in the Interlake with Gimli as its hub, and the reserves in southern Manitoba were populated by Mennonite settlers from Russia. The Eastern Reserve included Steinbach, Altona and nearby areas; the Western Reserve covered the Winkler and Morden region. Ushering in immigrants was an important signal that Manitoba not only tolerated, but nurtured differing religious and cultural backgrounds, and recognized the important contribution that the new arrivals would make to the province.

The tide of immigrants who came under Greenway's government accelerated with Clifford Sifton's move to Ottawa as a member of Parliament in 1896, and his vigorous promotion of

---

[28] Wilson, *Thomas Greenway*, p. 11.

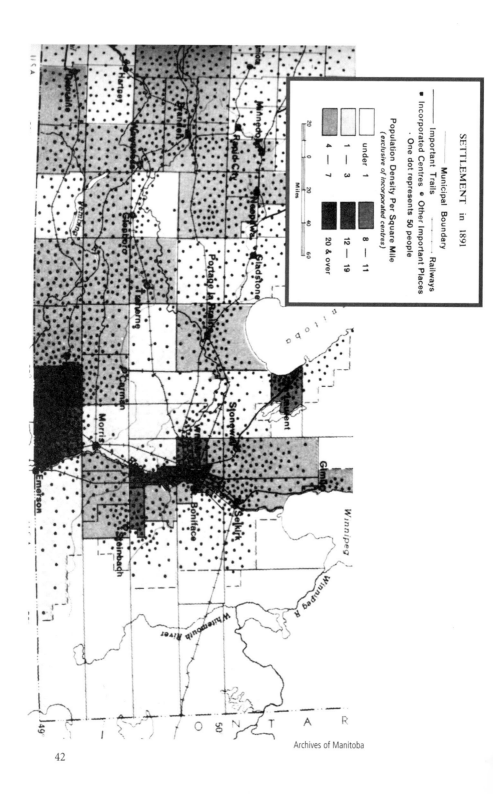

SETTLEMENT in 1891

Municipal Boundary
Important Trails ———— Railways
■ Incorporated Centres ● Other Important Places
. One dot represents 50 people

Population Density Per Square Mile
(exclusive of incorporated centres)

under 1	8 — 11
1 — 3	12 — 19
4 — 7	20 & over

Archives of Manitoba

immigration to Western Canada. In subsequent years, Liberals would encourage and welcome the diverse groups of people who came to Manitoba seeking a new life. Many immigrants were rural folk who came to cobble together a future in the province's unforgiving climate; in 1891, seventy per cent of the new arrivals settled on farms. Some, like the Hutterites, who fled to Canada from the United States to escape persecution as conscientious objectors during World War I, came for religious reasons. Out of the efforts of the immigrants would come a remarkable cooperative approach to building a province, forging much of the spirit and values still embraced by Manitobans.

The rapid population growth in Manitoba was not without its opponents. Hugh John Macdonald, the Conservative leader going into the 1899 election, dwelt on this in his campaign, leading the attack on ethnic minorities or "foreigners" who were arriving in large numbers. This wave of antagonism was one factor influencing the outcome of the election in 1899, when Greenway's government was defeated.

By the end of his tenure as premier, the increase in immigration and the tax base of the province had allowed for a dramatic increase in funds for education, health, agriculture, and aid for municipal governments and public works. It was an enviable track record. As was reported several years afterwards, "It was unquestionably a surprise to many, when in December 1899 [Greenway] the man who for twelve years had commanded the strongest provincial government in the Dominion was overthrown." [29]

After the defeat in 1899, Greenway continued as Liberal leader and leader of the opposition in the Manitoba Legislature. Horace Chevrier, sitting beside him in the legislature later commented: "I saw there how his personality towered high ... As a speaker he was weighty ... as a debater he was forceful and compelling." [30]

Then, with the federal election of 1904, "he could not resist the appeal to stand as the candidate of a government whose chief policies were better railway service for the west and a moderate customs tariff. [He was successful—being elected MP for Lisgar] His advent on the scene in Ottawa caused much interest. He carried his age with remarkable serenity." [31]

---

[29] Press clippings in the Manitoba Legislature files, including those from Winnipeg and Ottawa at the time of Greenway's death.

[30] Op. cit.

[31] Op. cit.

While in the House of Commons:

Mr. Greenway was universally esteemed at the capital as one of the strong men of parliament. Though he spoke seldom, he was regarded as one of the debaters of the House, having a forceful style and only participating in debate on questions with which experience and investigation had made him an authority. Therefore, the announcement that he would speak always filled the chamber. He was even more esteemed in the councils of this party, where his ripe judgment and practical mind gave his opinions an authoritative weight which few other members of the House could command. His sterling integrity, recognized by all the members, added weight to any advice which he gave.[32]

In 1908, he was appointed a railway commissioner. His reaction: "His strong rugged features were wreathed with [a] smile". He was pleased as were others who felt he could make a contribution. But unfortunately, very shortly afterwards he had a severe attack of asthma. It "was of such a severe character that Mr. Greenway had not been able to sleep in his bed for a fortnight. He simply reclined in a chair."

Then, on October 30th, tragedy struck.

At 3:30 this morning there was a fire on Sparks street immediately opposite the window of the room which Mr. Greenway occupied [at the Windsor Hotel]. The excitement of the bells and engines, the shouting and the crowds led the old gentleman to go to the window and watch the proceedings and brought on another attack of asthma of such a severe character that with his weakened heart Mr. Greenway passed away at 7 a.m.[33]

The eulogies and tributes poured in. Widely known and universally respected, Greenway was admired for his unquestionable strength of will and tenacity. He was praised as a man of exceptional administrative ability who ably guided the destinies of his province.

---

[32] Op. cit.

[33] Op. cit.

"He was remembered as a man of sincerity with a kindly heart, urbane to friend or foe alike. And although he was not fond of the sound of his own voice, he was a charismatic speaker who, in his vigorous days, was one of the best political speakers the west has ever known," Theodore A. Burrows was quoted in the *Free Press* as saying following Greenway's death.

His old friend and colleague, Clifford Sifton, fondly remembered him this way in the same newspaper:

> I was perhaps more intimate personally with Mr. Greenway than any of his late colleagues, and our relations were always of the warmest possible description, especially during the last three or four years ... He was a man without much literary polish or accomplishment, but was full of hard, practical common-sense and was, in nearly every instance moved to his action in public matters from patriotic motives ... I do not think there is a province in Canada that has had a more honest, economical and progressive government than the province of Manitoba during Mr. Greenway's premiership. He was especially noted for his consistent sympathy with everything pertaining to the interests of the farming community. He was a natural sympathizer with popular rights, and a natural enemy of monopoly in every form.

And Thomas J. Johnson, a prominent Manitoban, described him in the *Free Press* as:

> the dreamer, the visionary, the driving power ... a true leader of the people ... he looked not for personal aggrandizement, but for power to build and make changes. Farming, the lifeblood of the nation, was his main concern. Everything else, immigration, the railway, education, these were all to support his farmers.[34]

---

[34] Op. cit.

Archives of Manitoba

Tobias C. Norris

4

Putting Manitoba Ahead

1908-1922

Tobias C. Norris and Nellie McClung

*"It was a bonny fight—a knockdown and drag-out fight,
but it united the women of Manitoba in a great cause. I
never felt such unity of purpose and I look on these days
with great satisfaction. We really believed we were about
to achieve a new world."* [1]

—Nellie L. McClung, 1945

AFTER THE ELECTION LOSS OF 1899, Greenway stayed on as head
of the party for the next several years, providing important opposition to the government. But his leadership was no longer inspired
and it was only a matter of time before he left provincial politics.
In 1904, he ran federally, successfully becoming a member of
Parliament in Lisgar constituency. The rebuilding of the platform
and the organization of the Liberal Party in Manitoba took fifteen
years. This chapter is the story of that rebuilding, of people, organization, platform and partnerships. It is the story of one of the
most action-oriented, future-thinking administrations in the
history of Manitoba.

---

[1] Candace Savage, *Our Nell: A Scrapbook Biography of Nellie McClung,* (Western Producer
Prairie Books, 1979) p. 105.

After Greenway's departure, rural lawyer Charles J. Mickle was chosen as parliamentary leader. Mickle had been elected the MLA for Birtle in 1888, and served in the cabinet as provincial secretary from 1896–1900. In March 1906, a leadership and policy convention was convened where Edward Brown, mayor of Portage la Prairie, emerged as the new head of the party.

At the same convention, the delegates began to define the Liberal approach to some of the critical issues of the day. One of these was the need for compulsory school attendance to ensure that the increasing advantages of education would be available to all, and to provide young Manitobans with a better understanding of their province and their country. The Conservatives, under Rodmond Roblin, were clearly opposed and declared they would never allow the Schools Question—public funding for separate Roman Catholic Schools—to be reopened. Yet unilateral education was one of the elements of the new Liberal Platform and over the next several years it would emerge as an important commitment in the efforts to build the party and to become the government once again.

In the election of 1907, much of the Liberal platform was too similar to that of the Conservatives, and Brown failed to generate sufficient popular appeal. Roblin successfully characterized Brown as a kindergarten politician, and succeeded in persuading the electorate that the novice leader was not ready to govern. The Conservatives won twenty-eight of forty-one ridings and Brown lost his seat. When it was clear that he could not be an effective leader without a voice in the legislature, Brown resigned, and in 1909, moved to Winnipeg to open Edward Brown and Company, financial brokers, which he headed until 1942. He would return to provincial politics (representing The Pas) in 1915, and serve ably as provincial treasurer from 1915 to 1922.

After Brown's resignation, the leadership was offered to Tobias Crawford Norris, MP for Lansdowne. Of Irish descent, Norris was born on September 5, 1861 in Brampton, Ontario, and came to Manitoba to homestead in the Griswold area in the early 1890s. He operated a livery stable, traded horses, sang in the Griswold choir and became one of the very best auctioneers of his day.

He was comfortable in front of crowds. He spoke rapidly, as auctioneers must, and yet clearly and unaffectedly as more of them should. Most important from the point of view of those who hired him for their sales, he knew the appropriate price of machinery, land and especially livestock, and he was frequently able to 'work' that price from his audience without offending anyone in the process. [2]

His ability to mix well with people was not limited to auctions. Afterwards, 'Toby' or 'Crawford' as he was sometimes called, might mix and laugh and talk with his listeners, and maybe have a social drink or two. [3]

Smooth in his appearance and demeanour, yet caring, patient and persevering, Norris had the ability to bring good people together. He was elected councillor in the rural municipality of Sifton, and was successful in winning a provincial seat in 1896. At the time of the defeat of the Greenway government three years later, Norris was one of the survivors. He lost in 1905, but was re-elected in 1907, 1910 and 1914. Friendly and outgoing, with a wonderful a sense of humour, he soon gained stature as an orator in the legislature.

Norris would spend sixteen years in provincial politics before becoming premier, serving his apprenticeship, and building the team, the policies and the bridges with activist groups that were needed for electoral success. Initially, he had a small caucus, including such able men as Thomas Johnson, Valentine Winkler, Dr. R.S. Thornton and Dr. J.W. Armstrong.

Johnson, the first lawyer in Canada of Icelandic descent, served on the Winnipeg School Board in 1904, and was elected as an MLA in 1907. He became the minister of Public Works in 1915, and in 1917, the attorney general. He served in the Norris cabinet and was also the first Icelander to become a cabinet minister in a government in Canada. Winkler would go on to be minister of Agriculture; Armstrong, minister of Health, and Thornton, minister of Education. Gradually, these men mounted an increasingly effective opposition, ably attacking the growing political and financial corruption of the Conservative administration.

With Norris as leader, progress was made in the election of 1910, but Roblin, grandfather to the later Premier Duff Roblin, was still popular with the public. Manitoba was benefiting from large numbers of new immigrants, many of whom came to the province riding the crest begun by the efforts of Greenway and Sifton.

After the 1910 election, rebuilding the Liberal Party proceeded more quickly. The party was forward thinking and attractive to young people who could see that the laws and customs of a

---

[2]   Morris Mott, University of Brandon, "A Biography of Tobias Norris", an unpublished paper prepared for a forthcoming collection of articles on Manitoba's premiers, p. 38

[3]   Mott, Loc.cit.

predominantly rural society needed to be reshaped to meet the needs of an industrial society and of industrialized agriculture.

It was an especial challenge to the Conservative Party … [and to] the leaders of the Conservative party and the Roblin administration. They were all hard-headed, practical men who took life as they found it, were sceptical of reform and, with the possible exception of the Premier, indifferent to idealism. They could not fully respond to the new spirit of the times. [4]

In 1912, twenty-one-year-old college student Howard Winkler, the son of Valentine Winkler, wrote to a friend, "The Liberals have a fine platform. This province is fifty years behind the times in many ways, and the Liberals, if elected, will have to overwork their session to crowd in all their bills, including 'Compulsory Education', 'Initiative for Referendum' and 'Single Tax'." [5]

A big part of this new spirit was the involvement of women in the political debate. Among the group of crusaders was Nellie McClung. In 1880, Nellie (Helen) Mooney, age six, had come with her family from Ontario to Wawanesa, Manitoba. She grew up walking in the furrows behind her father as he broke the sod, and by the age of twelve, she was trapping mink. Early on, she began to question the dogma of the day that didn't allow young women to compete in races with boys.

Among the formative experiences of her youth was the time she first learned that women could not vote. Another was a neighbourhood picnic where a normally well-behaved young man drank too much alcohol and caused a normally well-behaved team of oxen to stampede across the field, narrowly missing nine-year-old Nellie and a baby in her charge. The frightening experience may have been the genesis of her lifelong advocacy for the temperance movement, which sought to ban the sale of liquor.

Impetuous, headstrong, adventurous and exuberant, she rebelled against constraints on women, and against her mother's Scottish thrift. At age sixteen, after five months of education in Normal School in far-away Winnipeg, she took her first assignment

---

[4]   Morton, *Manitoba History*, p. 336.

[5]   Irvin J.Kroeker, *The Papers of Howard Winkler*, (Altona, Friesens, 1999), p. 54. Howard Winkler, then attending Manitoba Agricultural College and living at 923 Dorchester St. in Winnipeg, was writing to his friend Isaac J. Warkentin in Winkler.

as a teacher at Hazel School near Manitou.

There, Nellie met the local Methodist minister and his family, the McClungs. In time, Nellie would marry the eldest son, Wes, but, it was her future mother-in-law who initially influenced her the most. Mrs. McClung was circulating a petition asking for the vote for women, which Nellie soon signed and later attended a political meeting where Thomas Greenway was speaking. Greenway noticed the two women and commented that "politics concerned women as much as men", but he was not yet ready to take up the cause of women's suffrage. That would wait for his successor, Norris.

Nellie McClung grew in stature as a teacher, a storyteller, a writer and a mother. As the 1914 election loomed, she became increasingly well known for her advocacy of prohibition and of votes for women.

During the period in opposition, the party had recruited the major talents of people like Winnipeg lawyers, T.H. Johnson and A.B. Hudson, as well as C.D. McPherson of Portage la Prairie. With these leaders, the party convention of 1914 completed the work begun in 1910, and adopted a broad program of reform including:

> Direct legislation, a pledge to introduce effective
> temperance legislation if a referendum should
> authorize it, women's suffrage, compulsory education
> with allowance for the constitutional rights of
> Catholic parents.

The party also supported provincial rights such as the transfer of control of natural resources from Ottawa to the province. On many of these issues, the lines were sharply drawn. In response to the Liberal platform which included votes for women, Premier Roblin, sneered that it was supported only by "short-haired women and long-haired men".[6]

When approached at the legislature by Nellie McClung and members of the Political Equity League, Roblin's answer was blunt:

> Premier Roblin says home will be ruined by votes
> for women ... Straight from the shoulder, Premier
> Sir Rodmond Roblin yesterday told a delegation of
> women that he is absolutely opposed to woman's

---

[6] V. Strong-Boag, M.L. Rosa,: *Nellie McClung: The Complete Autobiography*, (Broadview Press, 2003) p. 396.

suffrage … Sir Rodmond's argument was quite unequivocal. Women's place was in the home, her duty the development of the child character and the performance of wifely duties. To project her into the sphere of party politics would be to cause her to desert her true sphere, to the grave danger to society. [7]

'In summary,' he concluded, 'I don't want a hyena in petticoats talking politics at me. I want a nice gentle creature to bring me my slippers.'

Nellie McClung turned and stomped out of his office. 'You'll hear from me again and you may not like it!'

'Is that a threat?' asked the premier.

'No,' replied Nellie, over her shoulder, 'It's a prophecy.' [8]

The women responded with a performance the next night at the Walker Theatre. Nellie McClung, in full evening gown and black cloak, strode out in front of the curtain. She was an arresting figure with short, black hair carefully curled to just below her ears, high cheekbones, straight nose, and calm, yet penetrating gaze. She carried herself with poise and confidence, developed over years of teaching in front of her school classes, and speaking before audiences throughout Manitoba. She set the stage with a voice clear and assured, noting that the members of the audience, "would have to use their imagination, as political conditions were reversed and women were in power. She couldn't see why women shouldn't sit in Parliament. It didn't seem to be such a hard job …" [9]

Soon after, the curtain rose revealing the women legislators, all with their evening gowns covered with black cloaks, seated at desks in readiness for the first session …

Petitions were first received and read. The first was a protest against men's clothes, saying that men wearing scarlet ties, six-inch collars and squeaky shoes should not be allowed in public. A second petition asked for labour saving devices for men. A third

[7] *Winnipeg Free Press*, January 28, 1914.

[8] Mary Lile Benham, *Nellie McClung: The Canadians*. (Fitzhenry & Whiteside Limited, Markham, ON, 1999)

[9] *Winnipeg Free Press*. January 28, 1914.

prayed that alkali and all injurious substances be prohibited in the manufacture of laundry soap as it ruined the men's delicate hands...

The pinnacle of absurdity was reached when a deputation of men, led by Mr. R.C. Skinner, arrived at the Legislature with a wheelbarrow full of petitions for votes for men. Mr. Skinner said the women were afraid that if the men were given the vote that [they] would neglect their business to talk politics when they ought to be putting wildcat subdivisions on the market. In spite of his eloquent appeal he could not touch the heart of the premier.[10]

The premier, (Mrs. McClung) then rose and launched her reply, mimicking the words of Roblin a day earlier.

I must congratulate the members of this delegation on their splendid appearance ... If all men were as intelligent and as good as Mr. Skinner and his worthy though misguided followers we might consider this matter, but they are not. Seven-eighths of the police court offenders are men, and only one-third of the church membership. You ask me to enfranchise all these[!] ...

O no, man is made for something higher and better than voting. Men were made to support families. What is home without a bank account? The man who pays the grocer rules the world. In this agricultural province, the man's place is the farm. Shall I call a man away from the useful plow and harrow to talk loud on street corners about things which do not concern him! Politics unsettle men, and unsettled men means unsettled bills—broken furniture, and broken vows—and divorce ... When you ask for the vote, you are asking me to break up peaceful, happy homes—to wreck innocent lives ...

... I may be wrong. After all men may be human. Perhaps the time will come when men may vote with women—but in the meantime be of good

---

[10] Savage, Ibid. p. 88–89.

[11] Savage, Ibid, p. 89–90.

cheer … We will try to the best of our ability to conduct the affairs of the province and prove worthy standard-bearers of the good old flag of our grand old party which has often gone down to disgrace but never [thank God] to defeat. [11]

The words of Nellie McClung created a storm, and as she talked, met and debated with people around the province, the chorus in support of women grew and grew until it reached a crescendo.

The 1914 Election

… [T]he election of 1914 was the hardest fought and most evenly contested in the history of Manitoba … It was a contest between the past and the future, and the past was strong and deeply entrenched. [12]

In 1914, redistribution of constituencies had increased the number of seats in the legislature to forty-nine. Many individuals and organizations publicly supported Norris and the Liberal Party, including:

… [T]he Grain Grower's Association, the temperance organizations, the Orange Order, now formally demanding the abolition of the Compromise of 1897, and the Political Equality League. Dr. C.W. Gordon [Ralph Connor], a leader of the temperance movement, openly called for the election of Liberal candidates. Nellie McClung stumped the province for temperance and the Liberal party. [13]

McClung was a wonderful example of a champion who worked diligently to elect a Liberal government in Manitoba. She toured the province, speaking with eloquence and humour at rally after rally. Her opponents burned her in effigy in Brandon and attacked her integrity in several languages. The Liberal press hailed her as the heroine of the campaign, the great female orator, a power in the land, a Canadian Joan of Arc, the most noted living woman

---

[12] Morton, *Manitoba: A History.* p. 337.

[13] Morton, Ibid., p. 336–7.

in Canada. Clearly, she had a remarkable presence.

As well, Norris was an effective leader and campaigner.

On July 10, 1914, two weeks after the assassination of Arch-duke Franz Ferdinand of Austria-Hungary in Sarajevo, Manitobans voted as war clouds stirred in Europe. The Liberal Party had fought long and hard but was only able to win twenty-one seats to the Conservative's twenty-eight. In the previous election, there had been two Labour members, four Socialists and one Ukranian Nationalist. All of these were defeated. Manitoba, it would seem, was going to be governed for four or five more years by the Roblin government.[14]

1915

As THE YEAR 1915 BEGAN, battles were raging in Europe. But in Winnipeg, "Even sharper … was the contrast between the stark courage of the soldiers and the sordid corruption of Manitoba politics …. The headlines of the battle news were to struggle for space with the headlines of the Parliament Building Scandal." The scandal concerned the building of the new legislature, which had been started in 1913 by the firm of Thomas Kelly and Sons for a projected cost of $2,859,750.

Archives of Manitoba

The steel bones of the Manitoba Legislature rise from the corner of Broadway and Osborne in 1916. The realization of Frank Worthington Simon's Beaux-Arts conception would take seven years, cost millions in overruns and bring down a government.

[14] Morton, Ibid., p. 338.

Shortly thereafter, on the recommendation of the provincial architect, V. W. Horwood, and supported by other professional advice, it was determined to change from pile foundations to caisson foundations sunk to bedrock, and from reinforced concrete construction to steel and concrete construction.

The former change was well advised, the latter probably so, but the estimated cost of construction rose dramatically to about $4.5 million. In the session of 1914, the minister of Public Works, Dr. Montague, made this revelation to a somewhat incredulous house. "Pleading the nature of the session, Dr. Montague could offer but an incomplete explanation of this surprising statement, but [he promised] 'if I am still in this world at the next session of the Legislature, every detail of the figures shall be furnished for inspection'." [15]

"Construction continued without question, and was only interrupted for a few weeks by the outbreak of war. But rumours began to circulate of faulty construction of the caissons and of slack supervision by the government inspectors." [16]

When the legislature opened in early February 1915, Norris indicated his intent to keep the minister of Public Works to his word and, "declared that there was no justification for the plea that owing to the war, the Liberal government members should forego their right to investigate and deal with public matters."

Roblin immediately shot back, comparing "the opposition leadership to the German chancellor". It was to be the opening salvo of a fight that Liberals pursued with vigour, convinced that the Conservatives' victory in 1914 had resulted from broad, underlying corruption.

On February 24th, Dr. Thornton, Finance critic, and Liberal member for Deloraine, delivered a searing attack on the high cost of construction and subsequent borrowing incurred by the Roblin government. In his speech, he reviewed the following facts, "that the permanent debt of the province on which interest charges have to be paid, is now nearly twenty-six million dollars ... that the province is borrowing money at ruinous rates of interest ... [and that] we have no reserve of money or resources—not a foot of land, not a pound of horsepower, not a stick of timber, not a piece of mineral, not a single fish to yield revenue to the province ..."

It was a damning indictment of the overspending and poor

---

[15] *Winnipeg Free Press*, February 13, 1915.

[16] Morton, Ibid., p. 341.

fiscal planning by the Roblin administration. It specified that the ownership of most of the province's land and natural resources remained with the federal government so that the province had no reserves to help cover the desperate straits into which it had been led by the Conservatives.

On March 11th, the Public Accounts Committee began sitting. The Liberals, ably led by A.B. Hudson and T.H. Johnson, pushed for a thorough investigation of expenditures on the Legislative Building. As the days wore on, more and more serious allegations and evidence came forward. In the *Free Press*, the headlines read: [17]

MARCH 11: "Contracts to Thos Kelly and Sons paid by government before work completed"

MARCH 12: "Contractors have had easy picking—Already $250,000 too much paid on parliamentary buildings—more revelations promised"

MARCH 12: "Extraordinary conditions are found to exist on contract"

MARCH 13: "No order in council put through on matter costing Manitoba Province over $800,000. Further remarkable admissions made in investigation before public accounts committee on new parliamentary buildings"

MARCH 16: "New Mystery Crops up at the Public Accounts committee"

MARCH 19: "Government Majority Blocks Investigation into Contracts on the Parliamentary Buildings"

MARCH 20: "The Million Dollar Mystery: Where is the Steel?"

MARCH 23: "No records covering payment of $800,000 are available"

MARCH 25: "Liberals run against Stone Wall of Government Vote when they attempt to introduce evidence of vital importance"

MARCH 27: "Several requests by Liberals for documents and witnesses refused in Public Accounts"

But the Public Accounts Committee, with a Conservative chairman and a majority of Conservative members, voted to approve the expenditures on the building and the supervision of the construction. The investigation was foiled, though it was proved later that the provincial architect, V.W. Horwood, and other civil servants had committed perjury.

---

[17] *Winnipeg Free Press.* March 11–April 1, 1915.

The committee was also foiled by the absence of
the inspector of the caisson construction, one William
Salt, who was in the United States at this inconvenient
time, on the advice, as it was later proved, of the Provincial Architect and a member of the chamber who
was also a member of the Public Accounts Committee,
Hon. George Coldwell. The Committee's report approved
the expenditures on the building, and the supervision
of the construction. [18]

On March 31st, persuaded by the mounting evidence, Liberal
A.B. Hudson laid out the charges and called for an investigation
by a Royal Commission of Enquiry. The government of Roblin,
relying on the report of the Public Accounts Committee, rallied to
stand against the resolution.

The same day, a *Free Press* editorial called for an inquiry,
concluding that the situation was so serious that, "the rejection by
the Roblin Government of this demand for an enquiry will destroy
it." [19] When the house rose at 1:20 a.m. on April 1st, Roblin was still
refusing to agree to an investigation.

Conditions changed overnight, however, for the Liberals
had presented their petition to the lieutenant governor, Sir
Douglas Cameron, asking for a Royal Commission to investigate
the charges. On the morning of April 1st, Sir Douglas Cameron met
with Premier Roblin and is reported to have given the premier the
choice of recommending the appointment of the commission or
submitting his resignation as premier. Today, this would be viewed
as extraordinarily strong action by a lieutenant governor, but at
that time, it was accepted.

Given the mood of the day, an election would have been
a disaster for Roblin, so he chose to proceed with the inquiry.
When the legislature met on the afternoon of April 1st, the premier
announced that the Royal Commission would be called to investigate the charges. [20]

The commission was headed by Chief Justice T.A.
Mathers, assisted by the Hon. D.A. Macdonald and Sir Hugh John
Macdonald. It began its work on April 27th, and by May 7th, it was
clear that the Liberal charges had substance.

---

[18] Morton, *Manitoba: A History*, p. 338.

[19] *Winnipeg Free Press*, February 13, 1915.

[20] Morton, Ibid., p. 341.

The Mathers Commission, "showed that the premier and his associates were up to their eyeballs in fraud, looting the public treasury they were elected to administer." [21]

As well, "Other investigations later revealed heavy overpayments for land for the agricultural college and in the building of the law courts, as well as a veritable thieves' paradise in the building and maintenance of roads." [22]

"Contractors had been overpaid and had 'kicked back' large sums of money to the Conservative Party." [23]

But it is to Nellie McClung that we give the last word on this episode. She had, in her speeches frequently compared Premier Roblin to an old ox at her family farm. "Mike!—old friend Mike! Dead these many years! Your bones lie buried under the fertile soil of the Souris Valley, but your soul goes marching on! Mike, old friend, I see you again—both feet in the trough!"

On May 12th, Premier Roblin and his government resigned, and the next day T.C. Norris became premier. In Norris's cabinet were A.B. Hudson as attorney general, Valentine Winkler as minister of Agriculture and Immigration, Edward Brown as provincial treasurer, Dr. R.S. Thornton as minister of Education, Dr. Armstrong as provincial secretary and minister of Health, and T.H. Johnson as minister of Public Works.

Initially, the new administration dealt with the fallout left by its predecessors, including auditing the public accounts. It was also necessary to have a provincial election, which was called for October 15, 1915. The Liberals swept the province, winning forty-two of forty-nine seats in the legislature; only five Conservatives were elected, and the Conservative leader, Sir James Aikins was defeated. The new government wasted no time implementing its campaign promises.

Fiscal accountability:
In the wake of the previous government's problems in administering public money, it was imperative that changes be instituted. Legislative and operative changes were made to decrease the likelihood of similar problems in the future, and inquiries were established, which unravelled the lurid and infamous details of the scandal.

---

[21] Terence Moore, "Growing Pains", in *Manitoba, A History, Vol. 2* (Great Plains Publications, Winnipeg, 1991) p. 127.

[22] Jackson, *The Centennial History of Manitoba*, p. 187.

[23] Mott, "A Biography of Tobias Norris", p .9.

Former Premier Roblin and others were indicted with criminal charges.

Improving democracy and achieving voting rights for women:
On January 10, 1916, at the beginning of the legislative session, a bill was introduced to provide the right for women to vote in provincial elections. At second reading, on January 14th, the vote was carried and on January 27th, the bill passed third reading. The subsequent level of enthusiasm was without parallel in the history of the legislature:

> When the third reading had been duly and formally given, the ladies who thronged the galleries, the men who were also wedged into the galleries and the members on the floor of the house stood up while the rich soprano of hundreds of female throats sang 'O Canada'. [24]

The traditions of the legislature prevented such participation from the gallery under normal circumstances. But these were hardly normal times.

> ... [T]he ladies, with much fervour, took up the rollicking strains of 'they're Jolly Good Fellows' in compliment to the members of the house who modestly sat down. But as soon as the last note had been sounded, the members sprang to their feet and not to be outdone in courtesy sang in return 'They're [the women] Jolly Good Fellows'.

Nellie McClung, unfortunately, was not present. She had moved to Edmonton where she would further the cause of women and women's issues as a Liberal member of the Alberta legislature.

In the 1916 session, Norris and his government also introduced other changes to the Election Act. These changes, finally approved in 1917, provided for closer checks on the conduct of elections and did much to eliminate the old evils of rigged election lists, plural voting, and ballot-box stuffing.

---

[24] *Winnipeg Free Press*, January 28, 1916.

1917

Improving education—moving to compulsory education:
The same day the bill to enfranchise women was introduced, so also was a measure to provide for compulsory school attendance of children up to age sixteen. At the same time, the government brought in broad changes to education. These included funding to provide for "a school within easy reach of every child", and provision for "Municipal School Boards"—the development of school divisions, which were the same size as municipalities.

In 1917, additional initiatives provided for the development of school libraries—"each teacher in every rural school in the province will be given a grant of $10 per year which amount must be applied to the purposes of the school library. This is the first attempt to start school libraries." Also in 1917, under a new bill, changes were made to the labour laws to enable, "the Bureau of Labour to fight for the protection of the child under sixteen and to ensure him or her the privilege of undisturbed attendance at school." Cumulatively, these changes had a huge impact on public education in Manitoba.

More controversial were efforts to end the use of languages other than English in Manitoba schools, resulting in a considerable loss of support among francophone, Ukrainian and other communities. This was one of the Liberal's critical mistakes and cost Norris dearly in voter support in the 1920 and 1922 elections.

Temperance legislation and referendums:
The Norris government was elected on a platform to hold a referendum on prohibition and to abide by the results. The temperance organizations prepared the draft legislation and the vote was held March 13, 1916. The voters, who included women for the first time, showed resounding support for prohibition, and the new Temperance Act came into effect June 1, 1916. It was an example of Liberal support for direct democracy. Norris himself was a social drinker and from time to time would go to the Royal Alexander Hotel with his friend J.W. Breakey, but he believed strongly that government should follow the wishes of the people and the Temperance Act was passed to reflect this.

The Norris government led the country in pioneering and providing for "direct legislation". A measure could be initiated by a petition of ten per cent of the voters and submitted by referendum to the whole electorate, with the approved measure being binding on the legislature. While this approach was ruled unconstitutional, the Manitoba government "stood by the principle of the measure and applied it when modifications of the temperance legislation were proposed. Through the application of its provisions the Moderation League in 1924 got its bill providing for Government control and sale of liquor." [25]

> In the first six months after the implementation of the Temperance Act, there was a marked reduction in the number of charges of drunkenness and associated crimes. But it was only temporary. Soon, the bootlegger was a common fixture, his wares easily if not cheaply come by, though they were usually of an inferior and often dangerous quality. The crime rate rose, and the incidence of drinking increased at all age levels. [26]

After several years of experimentation with prohibition, liquor was made available through government control, and the prohibitionist movement died out.

Public health—public nursing system:
In January 1916, the Provincial Secretary, Dr. Armstrong, explained his bill to amend the Public Health Act. Its purpose was, "… to reorganize the board of health and to start an active campaign against tuberculosis, infectious disease of all kinds, and the infantile maladies which in this province carry off a much more than necessary proportion of its children under a year of age." [27]

The new provincial system of public health was gradually extended, and in 1917, the Hon. T. H. Johnson, minister of Public Works, opened Canada's first child welfare station in Brandon, Manitoba. The number of nurses employed in public health steadily increased, and by 1921 there were fifty nurses in various stations throughout the province. [28]

---

[25] Margaret McWilliams, *Manitoba Milestones*, (J.M. Bertard and Sons Ltd., Toronto, 1928) p. 204.

[26] Jackson, *The Centennial History of Manitoba*, p. 190.

[27] *Winnipeg Free Press*, January 23, 1916.

[28] McWilliams, *Manitoba Milestones*, p. 204.

Archives of Manitoba

The bar at the Premier Hotel, c. 1910.

Social policy—Mother's Allowance for widowed dependent mothers:
Social policy during the Norris years was strongly influenced by
the efforts of Nellie McClung and her organization, the Political
Equality League, who had witnessed women working in overcrowded
and unsanitary conditions in garment factories in Winnipeg. The
members of the league pressed for changes. Major progressive
social legislation by the Norris government began in 1916, when it
passed the Mother's Allowance Act, which provided support payments to the widowed mothers of infants. For the first time, mothers were provided with financial assistance which recognized their
important role in parenting. In 1917, this was followed by "The
Dower Act, also the result of agitation on the part of the women of
the province … Under it a wife gets a life interest in the homestead
or the city home, and is also assured of her share of her husband's
estate." [29]

Labour, election funding, railways and roads:
The 1917 session established of a system of credits for farmers,
civil service reform, a Workman's Act, changes to the Labour Act
to protect children under sixteen, changes to the Election Act to
provide for disclosure of sources of funding and to prevent the
abuses of the past. In addition, attention was turned to the

---

[29] McWilliams, Loc. cit.

Medical School and the University of Manitoba and to school libraries. There was also considerable progress in road construction and public works, as well as a major effort to plan for the Hudson's Bay Railway.

Agriculture:
Under Norris, measures were adopted to assist farmers, including weed control, and legislation to provide loans to farmers to help them build their dairy herds. In 1917, the Farm Loans Act was passed, providing provincially backed, long-term, low-interest mortgages. Within two years, more than $2 million had been loaned to some 800 farmers.

In addition, the Rural Credits Act was passed, which helped fund the establishment of rural credit societies. Local groups of farmers, through their own credit, and with government backing, could make short term loans to farmers in their district.

During the war, the price of grain rose sharply due to the increased demand, but farmers' costs were also rising. After a record crop in 1915, the 1916 yields were badly hit by rust, and in 1917 and 1918, there were droughts.

In 1917, the Canadian government assisted farmers with a system of orderly marketing. A Board of Grain Supervisors was established to market the crop, preventing wild fluctuations in price. Farmers supported this effort, and its demise after the war was one of the factors which pushed farmers to get more involved in politics. [30] [31]

The University of Manitoba and its Faculty of Medicine:
During the 1917 session, the constitution of the University of Manitoba was remodelled to reflect its position as a provincial institution. The province was now responsible for the finances of the university, whose needs had outgrown its original endowments. A board of governors in charge of policy and finance and a council responsible for the direction of education was established. Isaac Pitblado, a prominent lawyer long connected to the University, became the first chair of the board shortly after the act was passed.

With three physicians in the government, (Thornton, Armstrong and Hamilton), the Norris years were favourable for medical

---

[30] Jackson, Ibid., p. 193.

[31] McWilliams, Ibid., p. 203.

education. Dr. Thomas Glendenning Hamilton, affectionately known as TGH, the Liberal MLA for Elmwood, piloted the necessary amendment to the Manitoba Medical College Act through the legislature, and in October 1917, with the transfer of its charter and land, the Medical College formally became the Faculty of Medicine of the University of Manitoba. Hamilton, a member of the Winnipeg General Hospital Medical staff from 1911–1934, had built his reputation for public service as a member of the Winnipeg Public School Board (1906–1915) in introducing fire drills, free medical examinations for students, and supervised playground activities in the summer months.

During Norris' premiership, the Faculty of Medicine, with increased funding from the Rockefeller Foundation and the provincial government, significantly improved its ability to provide the basic science teaching so necessary to a medical education. A building to accommodate the Department of Physiology, Biochemistry and Bacteriology was completed in 1921, and another to house the Department of Pathology was finished in early 1922. With the recruitment of William Boyd (Pathology), J.C.B. Grant (Anatomy), the medical school's 'golden age' began, and its faculty became renowned worldwide when Boyd's pathology and Grant's anatomy textbooks became the international standard.

Labour legislation:
The centrepiece of the 1917 session was labour legislation, including workmen's compensation, minimum wage legislation and legislation to regulate industrial conditions. The changes widened the scope of the Workmen's Compensation Act, and set up a Minimum Wage Board. The latter had been strongly urged by women's groups who had made a careful study of the wage conditions among young women, particularly in Winnipeg. "This, the first commission of its kind to be established in Canada, was given control not only of wages but of conditions and hours of labour, and has wider powers than have yet been given to any other minimum wage board in the Dominion." [32]

The City of Winnipeg:
In 1917, the government brought in a new Winnipeg City Charter to modernize governance in the province's major city. [33]

---

[32] McWilliams, Ibid. p. 203–204.

[33] McWilliams, Ibid. p. 204.

The scandals and their impact—events of 1917:
The criminal charges against Sir Rodmund Roblin, J.H. Howden and George Caldwell were dropped on June 25, 1917, due to the poor health of Roblin and Howden, but the scandal had long-term effects.

> The revelations of the moral obtuseness of party workers and even ministers of the Crown, of the things which were done to raise funds to fight the blindly partisan elections of the day, discredited the party system in Manitoba … the Roblin government had been subdued to what it worked in, coarse and completely immoral party politics, and that the Conservative party had been captured by its machine …[34]

There was a wave of reform, and the Norris government felt it had to be much less partisan than its predecessor. In the course of 1915, 1916 and 1917, it succeeded in implementing major improvements, which in retrospect, were remarkable, considering that the Commonwealth was still gripped by war. The legislation led the way for changes that were gradually adopted elsewhere.

The conscription crisis also came to a head in 1917. The prevailing sentiment in Manitoba was that conscription was necessary to win the war. Wilfred Laurier, the federal leader, opposed conscription, and those Liberals loyal to Laurier felt betrayed by Norris who was not equally strong in his opposition. The Liberal Party in Manitoba was split and hurt in the process.

1918

Reform of the civil service:
In 1918, a Civil Service Commission was appointed to fill jobs in the public service by competitive examinations and on the basis of merit.

Public health:
That same year, the government, concerned about Manitobans with mental illnesses, appointed Drs. Clarence Hincks and C.K. Clarke to make recommendations. Out of their report came positive action,

---

[34] Morton, Ibid., p. 345–346.

including the appointment of a provincial psychiatrist and significantly improved conditions for those with mental illnesses.

Hydroelectric power:
Hydroelectric power in Manitoba was first developed by the Winnipeg Electric Company with a dam at Pinawa in 1906. Following the construction of the Point du Bois generating station in 1911, Winnipeg Hydro began operating and providing low-cost electricity to those in Winnipeg. Manitoba Hydro, the provincial system serving rural residents, was established in 1918.

New Election Act:
A new Election Act instituted proportional representation in the city of Winnipeg for provincial elections. Under this system, the number of Winnipeg MLAs assigned to each party, was proportional to the vote they received within the city. Outside Winnipeg, constituencies continued with the traditional single member constituency representation, with the candidate receiving the most votes being elected.

Labour:
In an endeavour to prevent labour disputes, the Industrial Conditions Board was organized, with Dr. C.W. Gordon as chairman. In March 1919, an Industrial Disputes Commission was established with sweeping powers to deal with labour disputes and with various other matters, including the cost of living, unemployment and excessive profits. But "By refusing to nominate labour members to the five-man board, labour organizations rendered it useless, doubtless aggravating Premier Norris and his progressive government in the process."[35]

1919

The Winnipeg General Strike:
There is a certain irony that the general strike of 1919 occurred in Manitoba so shortly after the Norris government had introduced progressive labour legislation. Following the war, Manitoba had the most progressive legislation in North America. The Norris government had passed the Fair Wage Act and the Workmen's Compensation Act of 1916, and the Minimum Wage Act of 1918,

---

[35] McWilliams, *Manitoba Milestones*, p. 204.

which provided a minimum wage for female workers throughout Manitoba. As well, the Norris government had brought in the Winnipeg Trades and Labour Council, responsible for enforcing the labour legislation.

But the winds of change were blowing in Manitoba, winds that encouraged the movement for further transformation. Many women were still toiling in poor work environments and earning little. Large numbers of soldiers had returned home and were seeking employment. Wages in many positions had been kept low during the war, and agitated workers, eager for better pay and improved working conditions, realized that they might have to resort to a general strike—to ensure that their demands received attention.[36]

Civic employees in Brandon went on strike on April 29, 1919. Their action was supported by school janitors and teamsters, and other workers threatened to join. The City Council agreed to submit the contract to arbitration and within sixty hours of its birth, the strike was over.

The success in Brandon foreshadowed events in Winnipeg. On May 2nd, city metal workers went out on strike. They were soon joined by the unions in the buildings trades. Neither the owners of the machinist shops nor the building contractors would meet with the workers, and with no movement at all, discussions of a general strike began.

Such discussions emphasized the success in Brandon. Labour activist Bob Russell delivered a fiery speech, crying for "no more defeats", and almost all the unions within the Winnipeg Trades and Labour Council voted in favour of a general strike. On Thursday, May 15, 1919, telephone operators stopped work at 7 a.m. At 11 a.m., workers in many occupations left their posts. "Almost in orchestration, the trams ceased running, the post office shut down, restaurants were abandoned by their employees, even the elevators stopped [at the time elevators needed elevator operators]. Somewhere between 25,000 and 30,000 workers in both the public and private sectors walked off their jobs."[37]

Before the strike and throughout the labour dispute, Norris was involved in meetings with Winnipeg Mayor Charles Gray and with various groups and factions. On one side was the 'Committee

---

[36] Smith, Doug. *Let Us Rise: An Illustrated History of the Manitoba Labour Movement.* (New Star Books. Ltd., 1985). p. 35–54.

[37] J.M. Bumstead, *The Winnipeg General Strike of 1919: An Illustrated History.* (Watson & Dwyer Publishing Ltd, Winnipeg, 1994) p. 25.

of One Thousand', prominent businessmen and those linked to the business elite who were opposed to a general strike. On the other side was the labour movement and its supporters, led by the strike committee. The latter acted almost as a *de facto* legal authority and issued placards and notices that read, 'by authority of the strike committee'. Though it did help maintain peace and order during a very turbulent time, its actions displeased Norris.

Many women played important roles, both for and against the strike. [38] Particularly prominent was Helen Armstrong, a member of the strike committee, and president of the Women's Labour League, who was arrested almost weekly until the end of the work stoppage. She not only helped staff the relief kitchen, serving up to 1,500 free meals daily, she was also a strong advocate for better wages for women.

Friday, May 31, 1919, was a critical day. Rain came down intermittently that morning, as thousands of people, many of whom were former soldiers, arrived at the legislature to demand that compulsory bargaining be introduced to bring an immediate end to the strike. About 2,000 people entered the building. Another 10,000 waited outside. Premier Norris, his provincial treasurer and the minister of Education met the crowd. When urged by J.L. Wilton and others to announce legislation to enforce collective bargaining, Norris replied, "No, I can't see my way clear to do that. I think we'd better keep out of the fight." [39]

Norris was caught between his own progressive instincts and the strong views of rural Manitobans who were focused on the strikers shutting down the major market for their products, and disrupting the wheat trade. The government was heavily dependent on the rural vote and the rural Liberal members of the legislature were generally not supportive of compulsory collective bargaining. Editorial opinion outside of Winnipeg was much against the strikers who had made no effort to present their case to the rural public.

Strikers like Roger Bray, who had supported Norris in the 1915 election, now chided his reticence.

> In 1914 and 1915 we came to your support, and thousands of us voted for you as a strong-minded and

---

[38] Gillies, Marjorie. 'Women of the Winnipeg Strike'. In *Extraordinary Ordinary Women: Manitoba Women and Their Stories.* (The Manitoba Club of the Canadian Federation of University Women, Winnipeg, 2000) pp 59–60.

[39] Bumstead, Ibid., p. 44.

straightforward man. Those we represent are men. Those supporting the Committee of One Thousand are not men. That committee represents the same bunch of boodlers who plundered this province to the verge of bankruptcy … They have purchased real estate to the extent of thousands of dollars and have made money out of the innocent, while we were away over there defending the land we love. [40]

Feelings ran high as Norris tried to occupy the difficult middle ground. There was pressure to break the strike using military action but he steadily resisted this course, hoping for a middle approach—a resolution that would need neither compulsory bargaining legislation nor force.[41] At that time there was no precedent for a premier to intervene in such labour/management matters. But Norris's inaction may well have cost the Liberals the next election. He was widely viewed as coming down on the side of capital over labour, and this hurt his position among workers and the labour movement in Winnipeg.

The strike came to a head in June, and ended June 25th. Increasingly, the strikers were demonstrating over the lack of a settlement and on June 16th, movement was made towards an agreement between the aggrieved metal workers and their employers.

At the same time, the [Conservative] Government of Canada decided on drastic action. On June 17, the major strike leaders were arrested on charges of seditious conspiracy and seditious libel and were lodged at the Stony Mountain Penitentiary. The leaders were soon released on bail and a mall meeting was planned for Market Square on Saturday June 21. [42]

But, this demonstration was explicitly forbidden by Mayor Gray. When the strikers continued to protest, the mayor arrived with special constables who had been hired for this occasion.

These men armed with clubs, rushed the strikers twice. On the second occasion, they used their pistols

[40] Bumstead, Ibid., p. 43–44.

[41] McWilliams, *Manitoba Milestones*, p. 207.

[42] Jackson, *The Centennial History of Manitoba*, pp. 201.

against the unarmed crowd. [They later claimed to
have been fired on first.] One member of the crowd
was killed and another mortally wounded. Troops
from Fort Osborne arrived in trucks after it was all
over. The strike was broken and on June 25, the TLC
[Trades and Labour Council] declared it over. [43]

On November 21st, as calm gradually returned to Manitoba,
the Golden Boy was positioned on top of the Legislative Building.
Facing north, the statue looked to the promising future of northern
Manitoba.

However, the election of June 1920 was not an auspicious
time. A depression was starting to grip much of the West, and
with the return of soldiers from the war, there was widespread
unemployment. Manitoba was still reeling from the aftermath of
the general strike, and Western farmers were worried by their
falling incomes, rising agricultural costs, and a thirty per cent
increase in freight rates. They decided to enter the political arena,
and in January 1920, the Progressive Party was founded in
Winnipeg. [44]

Farmers ran in the election under the banner of the United
Farmers of Manitoba. There was not a uniform platform, however.
Some campaigned on a rejection of the other political parties;
others focused on the School Act amendments of 1916—some
opposing the changes and others arguing they had not gone far
enough.

Norris decided to fight the election on his stellar record of
achievement. "So confident were they of victory that the Liberals
gave virtually no attention to constituency organization and were
satisfied with minimal campaigning. The result was a rude shock.
The legislature had been splintered." [45]

The election ushered in twenty-one Liberals, twelve members
of the United Farmers of Manitoba, eleven Labour candidates,
seven Conservatives, and four independents. Norris continued as
premier, but now he presided over a minority government.

One of the pleasant surprises, from a Liberal perspective, was
the election of Edith Rogers in Winnipeg, an active advocate of the

---

[45] Jackson, Ibid., p. 201–202

[44] John Kendle, *John Bracken: A Political Biography*, (University of Toronto Press, 1979)
p. 27.

[45] Kendle, Ibid., p. 27.

Archives of Manitoba

Edith Rogers

Child Welfare Act, and the first woman elected to the Manitoba Legislature. The daughter of D.C. McTavish, a chief factor in the Hudson's Bay Company, she was re-elected in 1922 and 1927. Years later, in 1963, her daughter, Margaret Konantz, would be the first female member of Parliament elected from Manitoba, representing Winnipeg South as a Liberal.

Nationally, Borden's Conservative government disenfranchised German speaking Mennonites, affecting many in Manitoba. This unfortunate action was reversed in 1922 by Mackenzie King's Liberal government.

1921

A troubled economy:
The farm economy had done very well during the war; farmers were among the most prosperous people in Manitoba. Now, this was no longer the case. The report of the minister of Agriculture to the legislature early in 1919 had recorded optimism.

> The acreage under crop had risen to 6,000,000. The dairy returns for the year were $65,000,000 to be compared with a return of $11,000,000 in 1915, only three years before. The stockyards at Winnipeg had handled livestock to the value of $38,000,000.There was a new egg crop worth $2,000,000. Even the potato crop rose in value to $21,000,000.

But optimism was the genesis of misfortune. Farmers responded to rising markets with increased spending, even going into debt by mortgaging their initial holdings to do so.[46] After September 1920, prices started falling dramatically. Wheat that had sold for $2.85 a bushel in September 1920, was selling for $1.78 by the end of November, and was down to $1.02 per bushel by the end of 1921.

Worse, the crop of 1921 had been planted using steep labour costs and high prices of manufactured articles. Farmers who had gone into debt to purchase more land, found themselves in a hopeless situation.

> Many farmers saw their savings of years disappear. Others found their once free farms heavily encumbered ... Bitterness of feeling among the farmers was increased by the fact that some classes in the country seemed still to be prosperous, and that in some employments wages were still high. They believed themselves to be exploited.[47]

The Norris minority government lasted two more years. It increased aid to hospitals, provided free public libraries and made improvements in the benefits to veterans and their families.

---

[46] McWilliams, Ibid., pp. 208–210.

[47] Op. cit, pp. 208–210.

In other areas, its hands were tied, and only 132 of 379 bills introduced were passed. To add to Manitoba's difficulties, trade barriers
increased, as ten years of reciprocity ended with the United States.

In early 1922, Norris made a tactical error in aligning his
government too closely with the federal Liberals, which had made
several unpopular decisions. He lost support, particularly from
farmers, and in the provincial election that year, the party was
decimated with only seven Liberals elected. The United Farmers
of Manitoba claimed the most support with twenty-four seats,
and went on to form the government.

Norris was disillusioned by the loss of support from the
agricultural community he had worked so hard to help. He
resigned on August 8, 1922, to contest the federal constituency of
South Winnipeg, but was not successful. In 1925, he was acclaimed
to a seat in the legislature and re-elected in a general election two
years later. In 1928, the government of Mackenzie King appointed
him to the Board of Railway Commissioners and he served in that
capacity for eight years.

When Norris died in 1936, there were many tributes, but one
stands out. "My old friend 'Toby' Norris never laid a claim to being
a grammarian, but he had a rare grace of expression, a storehouse
of the unpurchasable thing—common sense and a modesty at all
times almost amounting to self-effacement that was charming." [48]

Years later, Margaret McWilliams would say of Norris's government. "Nothing, perhaps, in the whole history of Manitoba is
more interesting or stimulating than the speed with which, from
being generally counted as one of the backward provinces, the
province came to stand in the forefront of the whole dominion in
laws concerning social matters." [49]

Indeed, Norris led an incredible, innovative administration.
He re-established public faith in government following the Roblin
debacle. He introduced a wide variety of progressive legislation
including women's suffrage, improvements to the quality of rural
education, and the establishment of a Civil Service Commission
which recruited public service employees on the basis of competition. Considerable advances were made in public health and in the
Medical School at the University of Manitoba. He introduced the
Workmen's Compensation Act, established a fair Wage Board, made

---

[48] ref–MG-16 B2, a clipping from the *Winnipeg Free Press*, a tribute in the scrapbook of
Mrs. Ethel Hart.

[49] McWilliams, *Manitoba Milestones*, p. 198.

pensions for widows available under the Mothers Allowance Act, and introduced a program of loans for farmers.

A man of rugged integrity, Norris said, "the first essential of public administration is honesty. If ever the people choose me to direct their administration, I shall place honesty first." [50] And he did.

---

[50] *The Monetary Times of Canada*, 1915. Manitoba Archives MG13H1 Number 57 in G528.

Archives of Manitoba

Stuart Sinclair Garson c. 1945

5

The Father
of Equalization
1928–1957

Stuart Garson

*"Out of the politics of Manitoba during the Depression,
the political initiative came which resulted in the equalization of provincial revenues. Without equalization,
Canada's unity might not have survived. More than any
other public man Stuart Garson deserves the title of
'father of equalization' and the new dynamic federalism
which has thus far spared Canada any return to 'the
winter years'."* [1] —J. W. Pickersgill, historian,
federal Liberal cabinet minister

WHEN THE UNITED FARMERS OF MANITOBA upset the Liberal
government of Tobias Norris in the election in 1922, John Bracken
was asked to become premier. Bracken was the principal of the
Manitoba Agriculture College, and for his first term, governed as
leader of the United Farmers of Manitoba.

Eventually, Bracken began to consider a link to the Liberal
Party. This may have first surfaced in late 1923, and again in 1926,
but Tobias Norris would not join such a coalition except as premier,
which was unacceptable to Bracken.[2] After Norris resigned as an MLA
to take a seat on the Railway Commission in 1928, the possibility of a
coalition between Bracken's party, now called the Progressive Party,
and the Liberal Party, was again considered.

---

[1]   J. W. Pickersgill, Speech at the Symposium on the Great Depression, St. John's College,
University of Manitoba, Winnipeg, Manitoba, February 8, 1974, (Manitoba Archives).

[2]   Kendle, *John Bracken: A Political Biography*, p. 63.

Discussions of marrying the two parties involved young Liberal Alf Rosevear, and the president of the Young Liberal Clubs,

Murdoch MacKay

Winnipeg lawyer Ralph Maybank.[3] T. A. Crerar and Murdoch MacKay also played important roles. Crerar was president of the Grain Grower's Grain Company and founding president of the United Grain Growers. He was first elected as a Liberal MP in Marquette in 1917, but by 1921, had left the Liberals to lead the Progressive Party, which success-fully elected sixty-five MPs. How-ever, this effort was not as suc-cessful as he had hoped, and by 1929, he was back as a Liberal serving in Mackenzie King's fed-eral cabinet. His role as a lead federal Liberal in Manitoba, and his experience with both Liberal and Progressive Parties, enabled him to assist in bringing the two parties together provincially.

Murdoch MacKay was born in Boulardarie, Nova Scotia, and graduated from the Manitoba Medical College in 1916. During World War I he served in the Canadian Army Medical Corps and was discharged as a captain. He practiced medicine in Transcona for forty years, but in the middle of his career he entered the political arena, and was elected MLA for Springfield in 1927. He became the leader of Manitoba's Liberal Party in June of 1931, replacing Hugh Robson who had served as leader since 1927.

Under MacKay's leadership, discussions with Bracken contin-ued, and by February 1932, a joint committee had been set up with five Liberals and five Progressives to discuss strategy for an antici-pated election.

Meetings [of the committee] were held on the week-end of 13 and 14 February and according to Thorson the two groups worked "harmoniously together, mak-

---

3   Kendle, Ibid, p. 63.

ing considerable progress in the matter of organization for the coming campaign … Over the next few
weeks Thorson, Crerar, Hoey and Bracken worked out
the details of the coalition … J.S. McDiarmid, Ewen
McPherson, and Murdoch MacKay were agreed upon
as the Liberal members of the cabinet.[4]

Mcdiarmid, McPherson and MacKay joined the government
on May 27, 1932. The election had been called for June 16th. Initially,
Bracken had wanted to run solely on his record, however, his
new Liberal colleagues persuaded him to mount a campaign that
attacked the policies of Prime Minister R.B. Bennett and his federal
Conservatives. Bracken's speeches criticized Bennett's high tariff
and inadequate unemployment relief policies. At the same time,
he vigorously defended the efforts of his own government and put
forward measures to further reduce expenditures. He "pledged
the Liberal-Progressives to a non-party business administration,
to necessary financial adjustments with the least loss of services, to
the creation of jobs in productive industry, to security of tenure for
farmers and homeowners, and to an adjustment of the burden of
indebtedness."[5]

In forming the coalition, Premier Bracken, as Progressive
Party leader, was also able to emphasize his willingness to work
with other parties to improve conditions for all Manitobans. He
welcomed the participation of the Liberals and attacked the Conservatives and Labour parties for not participating. He once told an
audience, "The only political platform I have is whatever is best for
Manitoba, not just for farmers, not just for city people, but for all
the people without respect of class or creed."[6] During the campaign
Bracken travelled extensively throughout the province, leading the
coalition forces.

The Conservative and Labour parties, in turn, accused the
government of gross mismanagement of the province's economic
affairs. The Conservatives made outlandish promises to reduce
taxes and restore Manitoba's credit if they were returned to power.
The Independent Labour Party (ILP), under the leadership of John
Queen, was also critical of Bracken's approach to fiscal accountability

---

[4] Kendle, Ibid, pp. 124–125.

[5] Kendle, Op. cit., pp. 125.

[6] Kendle, Op. cit., pp. 125–126.

[7] Kendle, Loc. cit.

and what Labour called "inhumane budgetary policies", because it wanted more government spending.[7]

The efforts of the coalition were helped by an effective network of constituency organizations put together by volunteers from both the Liberal and Progressive camps, and when the dust cleared on June 17, 1932, the vote endorsed the coalition and punished the Conservatives for their failure to join. The Liberal-Progressives had received a strong mandate, winning thirty-eight seats; the Conservatives were far behind with ten, and Independent Labour had five. There were two independents.

Unfortunately, MacKay was defeated in his riding of Springfield, and was not able to be part of the cabinet after the election. Premier Bracken brought Liberals Donald McKenzie, E.A. McPherson and J.S. McDiarmid into his cabinet, and the Liberal-Progressive coalition government began to attend to the business of the province. But crisis was looming, for the Prairies were in the middle of the Depression.

The election was barely over before fresh disaster struck Manitoba. The Wheat Pools, established in the twenties on a rising

John Bracken

Archives of Manitoba, Bracken, John

---

[8]   J.W. Pickersgill, Speech at the Symposium on the Great Depression, St. John's College, University of Manitoba, Winnipeg, Manitoba, February 8, 1974, (Manitoba Archives).

market, had been regarded by most farmers as a success, but the drastic fall in prices made all three prairie pools insolvent.[8] Bracken and his government acted to rescue the Manitoba Pool.

Bracken took the unusual step of moving the address in reply to the Speech from the Throne, normally done by a backbencher. His speech focused on the crisis in wheat marketing, and during the session, he appealed to Ottawa to take an increased share of the burden of unemployment relief.

Prime Minister Bennett was unsympathetic; he told Bracken he must first put the province's financial house in order. E.A. McPherson, the new Liberal provincial treasurer, acted to further reduce provincial spending and imposed a two per cent wage tax, in addition to the regular federal and provincial income taxes. At this time, the "direct taxation on income in Manitoba was far and away the highest in North America. In frugal, moral Manitoba there was still no suggestion of repudiating debt and a high degree of skepticism of socialist or monetary magic."[9]

The year 1932 was noteworthy in three other respects. A massive fraud was uncovered in the handling of endowments of the University of Manitoba and the Anglican Church, handing a severe blow to these institutions. It was also the year of the Great Famine in Ukraine. When word of this incredible tragedy in the winter of 1932–33 reached Manitoba, Ukrainian-Manitobans were galvanized to resist the actions of overbearing governments and to defend individual rights. Thirdly, 1932 marked a turning point in the relations between Bracken's provincial government and Bennett's federal government. Bracken increasingly linked his government with the federal Liberals, and when the federal election was held in 1935, the Liberals won all but two of the Manitoba seats; those, in north Winnipeg, went to the CCF.[10]

Bracken continued to lead the coalition government until 1942, when he stepped down to become leader of the Progressive Conservative Party nationally. His replacement was Liberal Stuart Garson.

Garson was born December 1, 1898 in St. Catharine's, Ontario. His parents were William C.W. Garson and Margaret Annabel Garson. Stuart's father served for a time as a member of the Ontario Legislature for Lincoln County, supporting the Liberal government of Oliver Mowat.

---

[9] J. W. Pickersgill, Op.cit.

[10] J. W. Pickersgill, Op.cit.

In 1901, the Garson family came to Manitoba. Stuart's father was the founder of the Tyndall limestone industry at Garson, which was named after the entrepreneur. He also served as controller of the City of Winnipeg and was prominently identified with the establishment of Winnipeg's municipally owned hydroelectric system.

Garson's childhood was far from easy. As a boy, polio left him a permanent weakness in one leg and when he was thirteen, his father died suddenly, which led to the collapse of the family business. Stuart developed a strong work ethic, earning money for the family as a delivery boy, as a harvester in the fall, and in the summer, as a guide on Lake of the Woods. He was a keen outdoorsman, and maintained a lifelong fondness for fishing, hunting and sailing.

Garson was sixteen when World War I began and had friends fighting in France. Unable to serve in the military because of his leg, he received his Bachelor of Laws (with honours) from the University of Manitoba. He articled with the Winnipeg firm of Messrs Andrews, Andrews, Burbidge and Bastedo, was called to the bar in 1919, and practiced law in Ashern, Manitoba from 1919 until 1928.

Insight into Garson's life in the years following the war comes from a talk he gave to the Westminster Church Sunday School—what he refers to as an "amateur sermon". He was already developing his wit and wry humour, coupled with unpretentious sincerity.

> I can remember that when I was a boy there was nothing to which I had a greater aversion as the very sort of performance that I am trying to inflict upon you this evening, and possibly one of the reasons I stand before you now is that I made as a boy a resolution that I should try to deliver back to society the same quantity of platitudes and tommy-rot which I had been forced to absorb from it at one time or another. [11]

He continued on, using his time in law school to illustrate his remarks:

> Our laws are not, nor do intelligent lawyers pretend that they are, justice. They are merely the rules of the game (conceived, we hope, in the spirit of justice) whose main purpose is to secure order ...our only

---

[11] Stuart Garson, notes in the Archives of Manitoba.

hope of securing individual and social justice in this
world is by our manners, by the way we conduct ourselves in all those matters of fairness, sympathy, mercy
and good taste, where there is no sanction except that
which we impose upon ourselves … It is sincere [my
appreciation of the honour which you have done me by
asking me to address you tonight] because in no institution with which I have ever been connected have I
ever experienced all of those qualities of Christian
charity and kindliness which come under the head of
manners as I have used that term this evening, to such
an extent as in Westminster Sunday School. It is [note-
worthy] that an exile of 9 years or more may take his
place here almost as if he had never been away, and
since that is the way you have honoured me tonight
I must thank you sincerely for your manners. [12]

In 1927, after John Bracken heard him speak at a rural meeting, Garson was persuaded to enter politics. He ran in the election
of 1928, and was elected the MLA for the Fairford constituency.

Garson continued to practice law as a partner in the firm of
Messrs. Johnston, Garson, Forrester and Davison while he was an
MLA. Earnest, bookish and diligent, he had clear eyes, a fresh face
and a thick head of hair rising above his wide forehead, giving him
a forthright, yet sympathetic appearance. Studious and analytical,
as well as scrupulously honest, Garson would serve in the provincial legislature for fifteen years—learning his craft as a political
leader—before becoming premier in 1943.

In the legislature he was wise in considering fiscal matters,
but sympathetic to social reform. As was said years later, "How can
he help being sympathetic? He started work when he was 12 years
old. Poverty to him is not a phrase in a socialist textbook. It is a
bitter fact. But he also knows that all social reforms have to be paid
for by the people. Utopia cannot be purchased tax free." [13]

In the 1928 legislature, he was clearly learning the ropes. An
article in the *Free Press* of January 25, 1928, commented,

Mr. Garson, who does not know the rules of the
house yet, got up long after the proper time on a point

---

[12] Garson, notes in the Archives of Manitoba.

[13] *Winnipeg Tribune*, November 11, 1948.

of privilege. He said it had been said we suggested in this column that he chewed gum and or cough drops when he was making speeches. He seemed to think it important to make an explicit categorical disclaimer. Therefore all who may care to know it now know that when Mr. Garson speaks he does not use gum. But after all, as we see it, where is the harm in a strip of Wrigley's, if managed with skill and discretion? It would give a flavour to most discourses, and indeed so many of them need it.

In the election of June 16, 1932, Garson worked hard campaigning in his constituency. He was also courting Emily Topper, daughter of F. E. Topper of Winnipeg. Emily, born in Minnesota in 1903, had grown up in Radisson, Saskatchewan, and Moose Jaw, where her father worked in the grain elevator business. In 1914, the family moved to Winnipeg and her father established the Topper Grain Company. Emily graduated from the University of Manitoba, and received the gold medal in French. She then did post-graduate studies at the Sorbonne in Paris and in Grenoble, France.

Correspondence from Stuart to Emily provides a window on the campaign.

May 13, 1932:
Friday the thirteenth greeting from the end of steel. Hope you appreciate the typing [looks like the type or the typist is a little uneven]—Am waiting for a Jigger to come up from Ashern for me, and am taking care of my correspondence in the meanwhile. Started electioneering night before last. All of the situations I have investigated so far certainly need attention, but prospects in two polls look fair ...

Sunday June 5, 1932:
I was very glad to find your letter waiting for me when I returned home from a long trip to Lake Winnipegosis and the Waterhen River, since it offered a few thoughts as a respite from the worries of the electioneering I have been going through.
I went to the Waterhen Poll by motor instead of aeroplane or boat. I had to pass through Winnipeg each way, Going west I was in the City for only a few hours. Coming back on Wednesday last I was in the

City over-night. I worked until about 10 p.m. at some things that simply had to be done while I was in the city—telephone calls regarding politics etc.—I called you up at this time, but the maid said that you were at the theatre, and I did not leave my number, as I had just finished a 900-mile round trip by motor and canoe with very little sleep between whiles and was 'out' on my feet. So I went to bed early, and started out the next morning at 7 a.m. for Ashern.

Tell your father that George Adam, the trader at the Indian Reserve on the shore of Waterhen Lake has tomato plants in bloom already, and watermelon and muskmelon forming the second leaves ...

I had a very interesting trip as I was with Dane McCarthy the member for Ste. Rose de Lac, who is a Catholic, and was introduced by him to all of the priests and monks and sisters in the country. We met one sister—an Irish girl who had obviously come from refined surroundings. She was at Skownan Indian reserve in the tenth year of her missionary work. Her two previous charges had been on the Bloodvein and Berens Rivers on the East shore of Lake Winnipeg. At the Bloodvein even the Indians moved away in the fall for the winter trapping and she was left all alone for the winter. She said that although she dislikes intensely killing anything, she was forced to do her own shooting because if she did not shoot she did not eat, the only meat that there was available to her.

This stretch of the country is a paradise for birds—especially waterfowl ... and I saw again for the first time in many years, birds like the white pelican and pileated woodpeckers ... It was a great trip and I enjoyed it very much apart from the political end of it, which I think was fairly profitable.

I passed within a mile or so from the shooting lodge of the Moncrieffs near Meadow Portage. They have certainly selected a great stretch of country to shoot in.

I have been immersed in political meetings since I came back. I have had some six already, and will have to have about ten more before the campaign is over. It is only on Sunday that I can get any breathing space at all. The work is particularly distasteful for me because I

dislike crowds so much and because I am so susceptible
to bores of which there is no end. However, there is an
end to all things, and even this shall pass away (and
perhaps yours truly with it). If it were not that one
cannot tell until the votes are counted, I would say
that prospects look very good ...

Your letter about lolling in the sun at the Canoe
Club makes me very envious. What would I not give to
be there now? Instead I have to go to a baseball game
and talk about politics and the calf that died, with all
and sundry along the fringes of the crowd. But I dare
say that I shall appreciate my rest all the more for having worked, and serenity all the more after turmoil.

Well, here's to it, and as I say to all the German
voters. *Auf wiedersehn.*
Stuart [14]

In 1932, Stuart Garson was re-elected to represent Fairford
constituency. A year later, Emily and Stuart were married. After
their wedding, Emily stayed actively involved with the francophone
community in Winnipeg and with French culture. The couple
had two daughters, Marjorie Joyce [Beam] and Eleanor Frances
[Swainson].

During his second term, Garson served as chair of the committee to investigate the closing of Provincial Savings Offices in
1932, chair of the Metropolitan Mass Transportation Committee in
1933, and chair of the Private Bills Committee from 1933 to 1936.

Emily and Stuart enjoyed their life together, as is apparent
from their letters, which are stored in the Archives of Manitoba.

For Christmas 1935 Stuart and I decided that about the
best present we could give each other, and incidentally
ourselves, would be a canoe, made to our own specifi-
cations. [They were both keen on the outdoors, and
spent Christmas holiday skiing in the Whiteshell]. So
a few weeks before Christmas we interviewed Mr.
Goodman in St. James and definitely arranged to
have the canoe built by him.

Later in May, Emily and Stuart toured Fairford constituency

---

[14] Letter written from law office of Johnston, Garson and Garson, Barristers and
Solicitors, in Ashern, MB.

in preparation for a summer election. Their timing was auspicious. Mackenzie King had won a Liberal majority federally, and T.A. Crerar, Manitoba's senior federal minister in King's government, was popular. Provincially, the Bracken government included Liberals and was increasingly seen as allied with the popular King government. Emily's diary for 1936, from the Archives of Manitoba, gives insight into Garson's life and constituency work.

> May 22, 1936:
>
> I hadn't been up in Stuart's constituency for nearly two years, so went along with him for the 24th weekend … We left here on Friday, by train, my first experience going by train, and I found it not too exciting. Stuart had to go onto Gyp [Gypsumville] to a meeting that night, and I got off at Ashern, met by Bob and Carrie. After supper we drove up to the nursing station at Grahamdale and paid a visit to the nurse Miss Johnson and the teacher Miss Haggarty, there. Spent a pleasant evening, had coffee, etc. then came home, arriving around 1 or so. We talked quite a while and it was after 2 when we finally got to bed.

> May 23:
>
> Stuart arrived back from Gyp on the morning train about 6, and crawled in bed with me. We slept late and didn't get up till about 10:30, to find Carrie getting dinner for the family and men working there … Carrie and I were so busy talking that we took a long time to get dressed to go to the Church Sale of Work, but finally arrived, made a purchase or two, and were guests of Dr. and Mrs. Walkin at tea. Stuart arrived too, from the office, to add his little, or big bit. We had an early supper at Carrie's, then left about 8, with Dr. and Mrs. W. and Mrs. Kahana to drive to Steep Rock, to a dance and meeting. We made it in an hour, the Dr. being not the slowest driver. Stuart got out at Snidal's store, and the rest of us went up to view the new house being put up by the Canada Cement people for their superintendent, then to the Nichols', the supt. We had stopped at the Nursing Station and picked up Miss Johnson too. Stuart's meeting had already started. It was successful, though not a very large crowd, then the dance started. When refreshment time came we had nice sandwiches

and lively cakes, and coffee. The dance lasted till after 1. We hadn't been sure whether we were going to stay at Snidal's for the night or go back with Dr. Walkin, Snidal's having asked us before, but in the end Mrs. Nichols said we'd better stay as they had made preparations for us and we did.

Stuart's correspondence to Emily indicates her involvement in the 1936 election campaign. At this time, the Garsons were living at 332 Queenston in the Winnipeg neighbourhood of River Heights. Emily's notes continue:

On July 27th, the Provincial election was held, and Stuart got an acclamation, the official nomination day being July 17th. It was not till August 21st that the deferred elections in The Pas and Rubert's Land were held, and Premier Bracken was re-elected with a real majority. There was great speculation as to who the new ministers in the cabinet would be, and various rumours in the paper—one being that Stuart was rumoured as Speaker, and another that he and Ivan Schultz were the 2 possibilities for Provincial Treasurer, and on Sunday evening Sept 20th, Stuart had a phone call from Mr. Bracken to be in his office at 11 a.m. Monday morning. And so, on Sept 21st, Stuart was sworn in as Provincial Treasurer, Ivan Schultz as Minister of Education and Doug Campbell as Minister of Agriculture and Marcon—without portfolio, and R. Hawkins as Speaker. Was it a proud and happy day for the Garsons and the Toppers!

The position of provincial treasurer (or Finance minister) had opened with the retirement of E.A. McPherson. Garson had learned much in his eight years in the legislature, and with his coalition perspective and his Liberal and financial background, he was a natural replacement. "Garson was an extremely able man, hard-working, intelligent, and quick ... he was a detail man and a compulsive explainer who, on any given subject, always knew more

---

[15] Kendle, *John Bracken: A Political Biography*, p. 156.

law than anyone else—even the minister concerned. In the House he was dry and serious and his manner gave no hint of his wry sense of humour." [15]

The Battle for Equalization

It was not an easy time to be the Finance minister. An editorialist later likened it to the position of Whig chancellor of the Exchequer in England, described by Sir Robert Peel as, "seated on an empty chest by the side of bottomless deficiencies, fishing for a budget." [16]

Following the election and his appointment to cabinet, on the Labour Day weekend in 1936, Stuart and Emily relaxed and went to McArthur Falls on the Winnipeg River with their canoe. Emily's diary, which resides in the archives, noted:

> One little island nearby, we landed on, and Stuart decided to go for a swim in his BVDs as we hadn't brought suits along. Got the fire going and coffee on, then he went in, and I finally decided to go in my undies too. Had a nice cool, refreshing swim, just got nicely out when a motor boat approaching in the distance hustled me, all wet, into my trousers and Stuart's windbreaker. Enjoyed our lunch on the rocks, then explored the island, but decided it was a bit small for our family of 10. Then off again …

His cabinet minister's salary allowed the family to purchase a new Ford. He and Emily took delivery June 17, 1937 and a few weeks later they motored to Ashern to attend political meetings and to visit friends. Emily comments in her diary, "We didn't sleep very well last night, as all the cows in town seemed to be congregated under our windows."

Garson focused on two goals. He had to deliver each annual budget and with Manitoba's fiscal circumstances there was no room for error. He was meticulous, keeping his eye on the long-term goal of better positioning Manitoba in federal provincial relationships.

As provincial treasurer, Garson immersed himself in the details of financial matters and federal-provincial relations. He worked closely with Bracken to achieve a full re-examination of the existing taxing powers and the need to shift responsibility to

---

[16] *Winnipeg Tribune*, November 11, 1948.

the federal government for matters such as unemployment relief and old-age pensions. Garson marshalled the information he needed and placed Manitoba's case forcefully before the federal government and the general public. During this time, "Bracken constantly sought his advice, and gave him more leeway than any of his other ministers. It was apparent by the end of the decade that Bracken considered Garson to be his most useful and powerful minister." [17]

After the election of 1936, Garson represented the Manitoba Treasury Department at the Ottawa conference of the National Finance Committee. He persuaded Bracken to allow him to ask Ottawa to investigate the state of Manitoba's finances and review the need for changes to the existing federal-provincial relationships. Ottawa responded by sending three young men from the Research Department of the Bank of Canada to Winnipeg in January 1937.

Garson and Bracken had retained their own expert consultants: Professor Arthur R. Upgren of the University of Minnesota, Professor Jacob Viner from the University of Chicago and Professor Alvin Hanson, University of Minnesota.

Garson presented a long and carefully detailed analysis of Manitoba's financial situation. He pointed out that the BNA Act did not provide provinces like Manitoba with adequate financial capacity to provide social services, and that increased transfers were needed from the federal government. He explained that Manitoba's mounting debt was primarily due to borrowing for relief and social services. From 1875 to 1936, the federal subsidy to Manitoba, as a percentage of revenue, had dropped from just over eighty-eight per cent to slightly more than twelve per cent. He argued that the provision of unemployment relief should not be financed as a capital expenditure by borrowed money but as a current expenditure out of current revenue.

He also strongly urged that:

> … [T]he dominion government should assume the administration and financing of relief not only for reasons of efficiency and equality but because it would deal with a national problem by a national instrument upon a national scale, and could therefore be coordinated with national trade, monetary and tariff policies. [18]

---

[17] Kendle, *John Bracken: A Political Biography*, pp. 156–157.

[18] Kendle, Ibid., p. 159.

When the representatives of the bank looked assiduously at the situation, they reported that the provincial government was, in fact, stretched to the limit and could do no more on its own. McPherson had been very careful with Manitoba's finances but the province urgently needed increased interim financial assistance to cover its existing obligations and to cover the interest on its debt. They also noted that a thorough investigation of federal-provincial relationships was needed to bring about a long-term solution.

The Bank of Canada report resulted in a significant increase in financial grants to needy provinces. In addition, there was a general realization that something had to be done before provinces like Manitoba followed the lead of Alberta, which was at that time (before the oil boom) in such desperate financial circumstances that it had ceased to service its debt and destroyed its provincial credit. With continued agitation from Manitoba and other provinces, Prime Minister Mackenzie King established the Royal Commission on Dominion-Provincial Relations. First chaired by Chief Justice N.W. Rowell of Ontario, and later, by Joseph Sirois, the Rowell-Sirois Commission was mandated to look into the existing federal-provincial relations as they applied to finances and the constitution. But it was a difficult task, bridging the competing views of the country. Winnipeg's John W. Dafoe, one of the commissioners, said he was being asked "to find foundations for a bridge in a bottomless bog." [19]

With increased federal support, Garson moved to end the wage tax. He laboured over the provincial case given to the Royal Commission. Manitoba's nine-volume presentation was an important contribution to the recommendations in the final report.

Garson presented the Manitoba Treasury Brief to the Rowell-Sirois Commission on Dominion-Provincial Relations at Winnipeg in 1937, and at Ottawa in 1938, and took a leading part in the supervision and coordination of the Manitoba case before that commission.

The report of the Rowell-Sirois Commission was received in 1940. It recommended a transfer of taxation powers from the provinces to the federal government, with the federal government then transferring to the provinces a National Adjustment Grant to ensure that standard services were available across the country. For example, responsibility for unemployment insurance was transferred to the federal government in 1940.

However, Garson was disheartened at the Dominion-Prov-

---

[19] James A. Jackson, *The Centennial History of Manitoba*, p. 231.

incial conference in 1941, where additional help for provinces like Manitoba was rejected. He wrote to Emily on January 17, 1941:

> Darling,
>
> I should have written before, but I was working so hard and was so tired before the Conference started that I did not feel equal to writing ... and besides certainly did not have the time. Since the conference broke up before there was even any discussion on the merits of the Report I have been so depressed I did not feel like doing anything. It is certainly a heart-breaking ending to 4 years of hard work; and the worst part of it is that instead of there being any solution for our troubles they will become much worse than ever, because the Dominion owing to heavy war expenditures are going to cease paying any share of unemployment relief, which will increase our expenditures by $1,800,000.00 per year, and at the same time will have to further invade our provincial field of taxation and thereby reduce our revenue. I had a long session with Towers at the Bank of Canada today and am to meet Ilsley and Clark tomorrow morning, and hope to know better where we stand after my talk with them ... but if the facts turn out as bad as the prospects we may be forced into default after all the efforts we have put forward during the past 10 years to avoid it. Such a result will be nothing less than criminal. It will remove all incentive for any public man to be responsible and will vindicate and play into the hands of Aberhart and the rest of the wreckers.
> Stuart

By March, Garson was campaigning in the provincial election, called for April 22, 1941. In 1940, a coalition government had been formed of all parties, including the Co-operative Commonwealth Federation (CCF) to deal with the war. Now, the fight was tougher than Garson expected, because a strong Social Credit Party was emerging. Pressed for time, he wrote to his wife.

Ashern Manitoba
March 31, 1941:

Dear Emily,

Please forgive the dictated letter but I am on the gallop these days and I am right at the moment holding up a man who is waiting to take me up by truck to Moosehorn. The conditions of the road make organization pretty well impossible. I have been on the road steadily for three days, sleeping at farm houses at night and I suppose I have only covered in that time about 18 or 20 households, but I have tried to cover the important ones.

My cold is getting better gradually. Although my voice is pretty bad and I am a little concerned if it will be in shape for me to broadcast on Friday next.

Things look well in all polls except Moosehorn, and Ashern and they do not look very badly even there ... Mr. Kirvan, by the way, is going to support me and speak at my Convention which will be coming off on Monday, April 7th. I will be in Winnipeg before then, however ...

Stuart

Ashern, Manitoba
April 20, 1941

Darling,

I should have written before now but I have been so terribly busy and so tired that I have not been able to find the time. Everything was going fine until I made myself what I am afraid may prove to be a tactical blunder. Because Edmond Prefontaine had asked me to speak for him in a joint meeting with his Social Credit opponent and Landeryou, the Social Credit organizer for Manitoba, and because I had to decline his invitation owing to my having to attend my own nomination convention that night, apparently Prefontaine explained the fact that he had no supporting speaker by saying that I was to have attended but could not do so because of a previous engagement. [The Social Credit Party (SC), which had arisen in Alberta, advocated easier credit to individuals based on printing new money if necessary.] On the basis of this the SCs have been spreading all around the constituency that I had engaged to meet Landeryou and then

defaulted. Being perhaps too thin skinned about accu-
sation of this sort I challenged Toutant to come to my
Moosehorn meeting with any speaker of his choosing
and present his side of the case. Where I made a
mistake was in not settling at once the terms of
the debate. When we met again for the first time on
Monday night Landeryou insisted on our taking up
the whole time of the evening in this debate. With a
rip-roaring audience that jammed the hall at Moosehorn
to the doors I was not in a position to insist then as I
might have done previously on any terms more favor-
able to myself without getting in wrong with the
audience. So instead of giving Landeryou as limited
a time as Bracken had done—I think perhaps to a
degree on the strength of his reputation and prestige
as Premier—I had to give him half of the time at the
only meeting which I was having at Moosehorn where
Toutant had already had two meetings. The result was
that I found myself mixed up in a knock down and
drag out battle with as fine a demagogue as I ever hope
to meet. I think that I gave as good as I got, I gave
everything I had anyway and when we ended my voice
which had been weakening the last few days was just
much more than a croak. The meeting lasted 4 hours
and was listened to with great intentness and waves of
excitement throughout the whole time. It certainly gave
the troops a bigger thrill than they have had for some
time past, but I am very doubtful whether it did not do
me harm politically. The Social Crediters were out in
force and the nature of Landeryou's speech was such
that with jokes and wise cracks that he certainly got
the best of the cheering and the laughter … In any case
it brought the opposition out into the open, and it is
pretty formidable …

I am very tired and homesick no end, but it will
soon be over now, and I will be glad to get back home
again.
Your ever loving husband,
Stuart

The Social Credit Party had mounted a formidable challenge,
but Garson responded with a detailed document noting that Man-

itobans, under the Liberal-Progressives, compared favourably to Albertans and the Social Credit Party. It must have been effective, because on voting day 1941, the coalition won fifty-one of fifty-five seats in the province.

THE WAR YEARS AND THE 1945 ELECTION

FOLLOWING HIS RE-ELECTION IN 1941, Garson was appointed the minister of Telephones and minister in charge of the Manitoba Power Commission, in addition to his position as provincial treasurer. Garson continued to try to get better fiscal terms from Ottawa.

September 25, 1941
Ottawa, Ontario (Chateau Laurier Hotel)

Darling,
It is now 11:20 p.m. and Walter Herbert, Jack Pickersgill, Carl Goldenberg and B.T. Richardson who had dinner with Mr. Bracken and me, have just left after spending the evening in my room ... We again come home empty-handed. It is not that we have not made good progress, but simply that the Dominion is disinclined to come to an agreement with anyone until they have dealt with all ...
If I do say myself I think that I handled this work this time fairly well. Mr. Bracken left almost the whole of the argument to me as he had not had time to familiarize himself with it ... I had a good case to start with; and I let them have it with both barrels ...

There were more meetings in January in Toronto and in 1942, a four-year deal was struck. The agreement provided for the transfer of funds from the federal government to Manitoba and laid the basis for modern day equalization transfers. Garson emerged as a strong advocate for western Canadian interests.

Late in 1942, a federal Conservative Party convention in Winnipeg chose a new leader to replace Arthur Meighen. At the last minute, Meighen and a group of Conservatives persuaded John Bracken to become a candidate, disappointing many who had supported Bracken in his fight against the provincial Conservatives in 1932 and 1936.

Stuart Garson was chosen by the Liberal-Progressive Caucus to take over from Bracken as premier, and to lead the coalition. On

January 15, 1943, on the departure of Bracken for federal politics, Garson was sworn in as Premier of Manitoba and minister of Dominion-Provincial Relations retaining the treasury portfolio.

It was a difficult period for Garson, who, "with great skill held together the coalition cabinet of Liberal-Progressives, Conservatives and Social Crediters ... He insisted that all the ministers remain neutral in federal politics but indicated his own sympathy for the Liberal party by stating publicly that everyone knew where he stood."[20]

Garson and the coalition government continued to provide steady and stable government during the war and to spend cautiously. In 1945, the CCF, concerned about the effect its continued membership in the coalition would have on its provincial and national fortunes, withdrew its support and went into opposition.

"Garson saw coalition government as a means to ensure the numerical superiority of Liberal-Progressives in the legislature. This goal was very important given that Garson regarded Liberalism as the only sound alternative to "the doctrinaire views of conservatives and socialists."[21] As Liberal-Progressive premier, Garson decided to continue with the coalition.

Garson took over as premier in the middle of World War II, and in his first throne speech, the pressure and the urgency of the war were apparent.

> One of the first duties of the Provincial Government dealing with civilian matters in wartime, therefore, is to discharge its functions in such a manner as to make the least possible demand upon the material and the plant and the manpower of the nation. That course my Government has endeavoured to the utmost of its ability to pursue by consistent economy and by delaying maintenance whenever it has been possible to do so without excessive loss.[22]

Much of the remainder of the throne speech dealt with areas where the provincial government was assisting the federal government in the war effort. In addition, there was recognition of the

---

[20] J. W. Pickersgill, *Seeing Canada Whole*, (Markham, Ontario: FitzHenry and Whiteside, 1994) p. 128.

[21] Gregg Shilliday, (ed.) *A Distant Thunder: Manitoba A History: Volume 3 Decades of Diversity*, (Great Plains, Winnipeg 1995) p. 39.

[22] Journals of the Manitoba Legislative Assembly, 1943 p. 8.

need to prepare for the war's end, including rural electrification and further legislation dealing with employer-employee relationships and collective bargaining.

Jack Pickersgill, a senior civil servant at the federal level who was intimately familiar with federal-provincial relations during this period, commented on Garson's vision some years later.

> On the purely provincial plain, his outstanding achievement was the electrification of rural Manitoba … one of the most successful and economic operations of its kind in the world. [This]would not have happened if Garson as Provincial Treasurer and Premier had not managed the provincial finances with such prudence that Manitoba moved from the edge of bankruptcy in 1936, to freedom from any net provincial debt … in 1948.[23]

As early as 1943, Premier Garson was concerned about the development of a plan to provide health insurance to Manitobans. Letters in the Manitoba Archives dated 1943 and 1944, to Mr. V.R. Smith, General Manager of the Confederation Life Association, discuss how to implement a plan for health insurance. One of the issues was funding the program, since the responsibility for health was provincial, and the funding capacity was greater at the federal level. In his letter of June 16, 1943, Garson says:

> So far as the Dominion Government is concerned I am wondering whether your suggestion could not be objected to upon the ground that if the financial responsibility is left with the Dominion Government and the administrative responsibility with the province, the result will be contrary to responsible government in that the provinces will be spending funds which they have not had the responsibility for raising in taxation.

In the years since the implementation of the Canadian Medicare program, this has continued to be one of the critical issues—how to keep provinces from the tendency to spend money much more freely when it is raised in taxes by the federal government—and how the federal government can ensure all health care money is spent wisely when it is not responsible for administration.

---

[23] Pickersgill 1978—comments recorded in Ottawa and transcribed at Queen's University November 1978.

Garson's increased duties as premier made family life more difficult. In 1943, he wrote to Emily while travelling to Ottawa:

Friday (en route) Canadian National

Darling,
When I came to last night I recalled that I had never said a word about our anniversary yesterday and had left you to celebrate it with sick children and a callous husband who doesn't even remember until after he had said goodbye to mention our anniversary…
Stuart

Emily replied:

Monday afternoon:

Dear Stuart,
Received your letter written on the train this morning apologizing for forgetting the anniversary. You didn't need to apologize for that at all. I knew you had your mind far too full of other things even to remember the date. But when you get finished with your big job down there you can maybe take a half day off and we can celebrate it with an easy mind.
Emily—XXOO from me, XXOOXXOO from the children

Emily's letters inevitably cheered Stuart up. In one of his replies he writes:

I got your letter when I was feeling pretty low over the war news and just as you always do it cheers me up immensely. You always make me happy darling, even your letters. I don't know what I would do without you.

Stuart also wrote to his daughter

How is my little papoose today? I am coming home just as soon as I can to throw you up in the air so high you will nearly touch the sky. I am lonesome for you, almost as much as for your mother.

Most of Stuart's letters to Emily were handwritten, but on occasion:

[Monday March 29, 1948]

Darling
     The fact that I took a few days off with Dr. Bissett has thrown me behind in my work again, so that is my excuse for dictating—of all things—a letter to one's wife …
Stuart

On some occasions, it was Emily who travelled and left Stuart with the children. He wrote: "the motherless, wifeless family is getting along fairly well although life is a lot more hectic with you absent than when you are here …"

Sometimes, Emily was at the lake:

July 12, 1945 Thursday
To Emily at 415 Matheson St. (North)
(Granite Lake)
Kenora Ontario

Darling,
     I am getting along fine. As to the housekeeping, for the nonce, the house, to be perfectly frank, ain't being kept at all, but I promise you I will have an orgy of housekeeping before you return.
     As to whether I shall be able to get to the lake at all will depend upon events. Needless to say if I can get there I shall, but in any case I will come down to get you back and will try to take your Mother down if I can get away then …
Stuart

[There is at the bottom of the letter:]
P.S. from the office staff. We know why the housekeeping ain't being done. Our noses are being kept to the grindstone too but as long as we aren't included in the "orgy of housekeeping" Mr. Garson is going to indulge in, I guess we can take it. Best regards,
[unreadable signature]

There were two elections in 1945, federal and provincial. In the federal election, Garson found himself supporting the federal Liberals, in opposition to his former chief, John Bracken, who was the leader of the federal Progressive Conservatives.

Manitoba was, in fact, critical, and in the end Bracken was the only Conservative elected in the province. "In the election of 1945, Garson had kept the Liberal flame alive. Without the 10 Manitoba MPs, Mackenzie King would not have had a clear majority in that postwar election."[24]

In the summer of 1945, Garson was very busy getting ready for a federal-provincial conference in August and for a fall provincial election.

July 23, 1945
Legislative Assembly, Winnipeg
Monday 2 a.m.

Darling,
Just a note to announce that I have just finished dictating the first continuous draft of my conference address in 27 cylinders—a new record in dictation for me.
Stuart

A detailed, five-page letter dated October 4, 1945, was written to constituents of Fairford outlining the government's accomplishments.

The Government of Manitoba does not claim credit for this except on one count. By carefully handling the business that you have entrusted to us, we have kept up the standard of provincial services without increasing provincial taxation unduly. We have thereby enabled you to do your best in the midst of very difficult world circumstances.

This much has been done for the most part either in a time of depression or war when it is hard to get things done. So of course there is still much to do. Certain districts in the Constituency have not yet got adequate roads. Others lack roads, drainage. When we have got these districts provided for, we shall still have to take care of the gravelling of all our roads ... When

---

[24] J. W. Pickersgill, *Seeing Canada Whole*, p. 808.

first nominated I said that I would make no promises. That resolution has been followed ever since. People appreciate performance better than promises. It is on the Government's performance and my own perform-ance as your Member for Fairford that I ask you as a friend and supporter to use all of your influence and your vote to help my re-election on October 15th next.

In the election of October 1945, Garson's Liberal Progressive government was returned to power. A top priority was the federal-provincial financial relationship, as the tax agreement of 1942 was to end in 1946. In August 1945, the federal government called a con-ference with the provinces to discuss future financial relationships. Garson hoped that the Rowell-Sirois Commission report would be brought forward again, but the opposition of Ontario and Québec was unchanged. Under the federal government proposal, which would last for three years, Ottawa would continue collecting income and corporation taxes and provide to the provinces, in return, an annual subsidy of twelve dollars per person. For Manitoba, with a population of about 730,000, this would mean an additional $8.8 million. There were other benefits.

The federal treasury would assume the cost of old age pen-sions for those seventy and over, and half the cost of pensions for those between sixty-five and sixty-nine, and of a health insurance scheme. The federal responsibility for the unemployed employables would be extended, and the government could contribute to a fed-eral-provincial scheme of public works of a developmental nature in frontier and mining regions ...[25]

The provinces asked for adequate time to review the proposals. In early 1946, the conference resumed. "The federal government now raised its subsidy to the figure of fifteen dollars a head, an amount to be increased only with a rise in national income above the level of 1942." [26] Seven provinces were in agreement, but Ontario and Québec were not. The federal government decided to enter into individual agreements with the provinces, and in November 1946, Premier Garson signed a tax agreement with the federal gov-ernment, which was revised upwards in January 1947. Manitoba agreed not to levy income or corporation taxes, or succession duties, for a five-year period for a minimum annual payment of more

---

[25] Morton, Ibid., p. 450.

[26] Morton, Ibid., pp. 460-461.

than $13 and a half million, increasing income to the province by at least $5 million, five hundred thousand a year. Garson had achieved the fiscal fairness and justice which he had sought, and in the process, laid the basis for the present day equalization transfers.

Garson was in the nation's capital when the documents went through the federal cabinet.

> Chateau Laurier
> Ottawa
> Sunday evening
>
> Dear Darling,
> Just a few words before I retire. We have just been putting the finishing touches on our brief which will be presented to the Cabinet tomorrow morning. It really is a magnificent piece of work—I can say this without prejudice for I have had very little to do with the preparation …
> … Good night my love, time cannot fly fast enough until I am back with you again.
> Stuart

Garson had accomplished much in Manitoba, but what he still wanted to accomplish had to be done from Ottawa. He began to consider the move to federal politics.

> May 1, 1948
>
> Dear Emily,
> This is a very brief and hasty note written while I am waiting for Godbout to call to take me out to another function. The meeting was a knockout. St. Laurent, Godbout and I were each given the works in standing ovations and I could hardly get more than half a dozen sentences out without being interrupted by prolonged applause. This sort of thing tends to create in one the illusion that he can speak, but I have put so many Manitoba members to sleep to cherish such an idea for any length of time. I should think that a political campaign here would be a lot of fun. They miss nothing. When they responded so well I tried some nuances in English and they reacted nobly to them all. What an audience.

As soon as I had said two words of French they broke into vociferous and prolonged applause that put me off my stride a bit so I don't think I did justice to the really excellent script that you and Miss Vogel prepared for me.
Stuart

Garson was, by this time, very well respected nationally. At the 1948 convention of the federal Liberal Party in Ottawa, he was one of those carefully considered for Liberal Leader and prime minister. John Bird, Chief of *Southam News Services* summarized Garson's attributes in a detailed account of those who might be chosen by the convention to lead the Liberal Party.

Stuart Garson is not actually seeking the leadership, he is likely to be elected only in the event of a deadlock in the convention. If that arose, he could become a formidable contender.
A short stocky young man with near sandy hair, a round face, jutty chin, wide set blue eyes and a disarming smile that often becomes a school-boy grin, is one of the best 'outsider' bets for nomination to the Liberal leadership. He is Premier Stuart Garson of Manitoba.
Watching Stuart Garson, an observer would guess that he had just one eye on the Liberal leadership, not so much this year as next time the post changes hands, particularly if one of the older men, such as St. Laurent or Gardiner is elected leader in August.
Orthodox financiers often praise Garson to the sky because of the prudent, conservative manner in which he is handling Manitoba's finances, using surpluses to retire debt and so forth. But outside the treasury door, Garson is no right wing Liberal or near-Conservative. He is a strong believer in the co-operative movement and believes that co-operatives may 'save' the system from Socialism. Socialization of such natural monopolies as power and telephones does not disturb him in the least. But he is a thorough-going opponent of all-in Socialism. If Garson were Prime Minister of Canada, observers would look for financial orthodoxy in the nation's budgets so far as that could be combined with progressive ideas on social services

etc. There would be no violent turn to the right or left from Mackenzie King Liberalism.

… Personally Stuart Garson is a man of great charm. He works late hours in the office year in and year out, but now and then disappears to a hide-out in the lake district not too far from Winnipeg, where he comes to life again in the woods. In spite of a game leg which has caused him to limp slightly from childhood, he is a sturdy hiker and loves to walk into camp (which used to be a matter of some miles) with a packsack on his back and with little else for food but milk, specially milled whole wheat and the inevitable apple which he eats with breakfast. Garson is an enthusiastic fisherman, but, for him the delight of the woods is getting away from the telephone and undergoing that change of mind which spirits him completely away from politics and balance sheets.

If the Dominion Liberals are looking for a 'coming man' with accent on youth, Garson may get the nod.

At the convention, Garson was nominated, but withdrew in favour of Louis St. Laurent, who became the next prime minister.

Garson resigned as premier of Manitoba in November 1948, to accept an appointment as minister of Justice in the new St. Laurent government. He was sworn in to the Privy Council on November 15, 1948, and appointed minister of Justice and attorney general of Canada. He successfully contested a by-election in Marquette, which as the *Winnipeg Tribune* reported on October 28, 1948, proved to be to his advantage.

Mr. Garson is not an eloquent orator, but he is a sincere, sound and convincing man. He is chosen from Manitoba because he is that province's outstanding public man and also, because he does not represent a Winnipeg riding. Mr. Ralph Maybank, parliamentary assistant to the Minister of Health and Welfare, is of cabinet material, but he sits for a Winnipeg seat. Winnipeg politicians are none too popular throughout the west, possibly because they are situated too close to the Grain Exchange.

Garson was re-elected in 1949 and 1953, and he continued to serve as Justice minister in St. Laurent's government.

In 1954, Garson was seriously considered for the portfolio of Finance, and might have been promoted had it not been for controversy over the tabling of a report on flour-milling combines in 1949, and for his inability to "summarize and simplify a case. St. Laurent told me he feared that with all the business a minister of finance had to bring before the cabinet and Parliament, Garson's lengthy presentations might cause strains that could weaken the government." [27]

Garson had a well-deserved reputation as a capable organizer. During his service in Parliament he was chairman of the Committee of Attorneys General [first appointed to this position in 1950], which was established to conduct the first plenary session of the Federal Provincial Conference on Constitutional Amendments held in Ottawa in January 1950. He was chairman of the Canadian delegation to the Sixth General Assembly of the United Nations held in 1952, in Paris.

He continued to serve in Ottawa until he was defeated in the general election of June 10, 1957. After thirty years in public life he returned to the private practice of law with the firm of Johnston, Garson, Forrester, Davison and Taylor in Winnipeg, where he remained until he retired in 1965.

Garson did get involved in the 1959 provincial campaign and he continued to make occasional public appearances. In 1960, on the fiftieth anniversary of the founding of Ashern, he was in the community to celebrate, along with J.W. Pickersgill, who became a senior public servant with Mackenzie King and later a cabinet minister under St. Laurent and Pearson. Both had roots in Ashern and were good friends. Pickersgill recounts, "Ashern had the unique distinction of providing two cabinet ministers in the federal government at the same time. The central feature of the ceremony was the presence of Stuart Garson … I had not been back in Ashern since 1955 and was surprised that the village had extended into our farm."

In 1971, Garson was named a Companion of the Order of Canada. Garson was a member of the Masonic Order and Scottish Rite, as indeed were almost all premiers from 1874 to 1969. At the time of his death in Winnipeg on May 5, 1977 he had four grandchildren—Sara and Matthew Beam, and Eirik and Andrew Swainson.

Emily lived another twelve years. She died on July 18, 1989 in Kenora, Ontario, at the age of eighty-six.

---

[27] J.W. Pickersgill, *Seeing Canada Whole*, p. 412.

Jack Pickersgill summed up Garson's contributions:

Garson's ... constructive part in the federal-provincial conference and negotiations on tax sharing was more than once really decisive. Without a viable system of federal-provincial tax sharing and equalization it is hard to see how Canada could have escaped disintegration ... Garson should be counted as one of the saviours of Confederation. Tax sharing with equalization is his greatest monument. [28]

It is my considered judgment that no other Manitoban in public life accomplished so much for the province. Few Manitobans in public life, if any, made a more lasting impression on our national life. [29]

Stuart Garson is a part of the heritage of Manitoba and of Canada.

---

[28] Pickersgill—comments recorded in Ottawa and transcribed at Queen's University November 1978.

[29] Pickersgill 1978 –op. cit.

Archives of Manitoba

Douglas L. Campbell

6

Fiscal Prudence and Forward Thinking
1948–1961

D.L. (Douglas) Campbell

"... [H]is warm understanding of the problems of others endears him to everyone ... His boyish sense of humour delights his friends and his opponents—it is never unkind." [1]

—Gildas Molgat

Douglas Lloyd Campbell was an MLA for twenty-seven years before he was sworn in as premier of Manitoba in November 1948. He succeeded Stuart Garson as Liberal leader and continued the tradition of combining careful financial management with innovative thinking. He was a team player. "What he was able to accomplish, during his long period of public service, was due to team work," Gildas Molgat wrote in his unpublished biography, "Campbell of Manitoba". Quoting his subject, Molgat added, "my predecessors in office were part of the team as well as my colleagues in the cabinet, and House." [2]

Campbell was born May 27, 1895, in Portage la Prairie. His father, John Howard Campbell, and his mother, Mary Campbell, had come from eastern Ontario in 1890 to homestead at Flee Island, just north-east of Portage la Prairie.

At about age three, young Douglas lost the sight in one eye; the injury is believed to have occurred when he fell on the point of a pair of pliers. It was not an auspicious early event, but it may have been the genesis of his legendary memory. To avoid eye strain, he

---

[1] *Winnipeg Sun*, March 5, 1984, p. 10.

[2] Gil Molgat, "Campbell of Manitoba", (Manuscript in Library of Manitoba Legislature), p. 5.

forced himself to read something once and remember the details precisely.

Campbell attended primary school at Flee Island, followed by high school at Portage la Prairie Collegiate Institute, and two years at Brandon College in Brandon

Little is known of his childhood but one story does survive from his teenage years. He was walking along the road near his home when he met a man recently arrived from the United States. "Have you lived here all your life?" asked the newcomer. "Not yet!" replied Campbell.

At age twenty-two, Campbell—or "D.L." to those who knew him well—took over the farm. Three years later he married Gladys Crampton, a schoolteacher from High Bluff, just south of Flee Island. They had three sons, Keith, Terence and Craig and four daughters, Dawn (Mrs. Jack McKeag), Sharon (Mrs. Victor Naimish), Sonya, (Mrs. Scott Wright), and Dwili (Mrs. William Burns).

Campbell's political career began in 1922, when he was twenty-seven. A humorous story recounts a visit with a neighbour who commented on Campbell's impending jump into the political fire. "I hear Tidsbury is running for election. He's not much good. I also hear Toupe is running. He's not done much. And now I hear you might run," the neighbour concluded, eyeing the potential new candidate.

"I haven't decided," replied Campbell.

"Well you might as well. None of them are any good either."

With this endorsement, he ran in the constituency of Lakeside, as the representative of the United Farmers of Manitoba, a grassroots party which had elected several members in 1920. To the surprise of many, including the United Farmers, they received a majority. However, they had no leader and several of the group, including Campbell, approached John Bracken, then Dean of Agriculture at the University of Manitoba, to take on the job. After 1922, the United Farmers formally became the Progressives and then the Liberal-Progressives when they formed a coalition government with the Liberals in 1932.

Campbell won his constituency in successive elections, but remained a backbencher and continued actively farming until 1936. That year, he was appointed to cabinet as minister of Agriculture and Immigration, serving in that capacity until 1948.

In 1942, Bracken resigned and Stuart Garson became premier. Campbell was made minister in charge of the Power Commission, while continuing as minister of Agriculture and Immigration.

When Garson resigned as premier, Campbell was chosen by

his colleagues as Garson's successor. The following year, he was formally elected leader of the Liberal Party. He was re-elected as head of the Liberal-Progressive government in the elections of 1949 and 1953, each time with large majorities.

Campbell's years in cabinet had served as an important apprenticeship. He was thoroughly knowledgeable in all aspects of government and had a firm understanding of urban and rural issues. He was a formidable speaker; when he rose in the legislature or appeared before an audience, his words flowed smoothly and eloquently—usually without the use of notes.

As a leader, D.L. Campbell had a reputation for being cautious, thrifty and fiscally responsible. He continued the program of debt reduction begun by his predecessor. His administration facilitated the economic growth of the province by improving provincial infrastructure and by ensuring balanced budgets and competitive taxes. His government made a series of wise investments to extend the highway network and to complete the rural electrification program. Rather than providing grants to promote economic development, Campbell provided a healthy environment for business investment.

RURAL ELECTRIFICATION

As MINISTER IN CHARGE of the Power Commission, Campbell launched an effort to extend electricity to rural Manitoba. He began in 1945, by extending electricity to 1,000 farms. This was followed by the electrification of 1,700 farms in 1946, 3,600 farms in 1947 and 5,000 farms in 1948. Each year after that, another 5,000 farms were added until all the farming areas of Manitoba had electricity. By the time the program was completed, the demand far exceeded the initial estimate, and rural electrification had altered the daily lives of nearly half of the people of Manitoba. It was a major achievement of the Campbell government, and one of the major advances for Manitoba during the twentieth century.[3]

HIGHWAYS

CAMPBELL'S GOVERNMENT encouraged the improvement of existing roads in the province, as well as road construction, including the designing and building of the Trans-Canada Highway. The Manitoba section of the highway was one of the

---

[3] Molgat, Ibid., p. 6.

first to be completed, with a new, shorter road bed constructed from Ontario to Portage la Prairie. [4] Two new bridges spanned the Assiniboine River. From west of Sidney to just east of Brandon, a new and straighter route was employed; from Brandon going west, the old Number One Highway was extended over the Assiniboine River on a new bridge.

Highways 10 and 75, the main access roads from Winnipeg and Brandon to the American border, were built to Trans-Canada standards.

The "roads to resources" program in the north saw Number 10 highway extended north through Riding Mountain National Park to The Pas and Flin Flon. The south section of Winnipeg's Perimeter Road, as well as the erection of a bridge over the Red River, were planned, designed and partially completed by the Campbell administration. [5]

A Floodway to Protect Winnipeg

THE FLOODING OF THE RED RIVER IN 1950 had a huge impact on the City of Winnipeg. Much of the city was under water and large numbers of people had to be evacuated. To those in Winnipeg, with water swirling around their homes, there was no question this was a disaster. The Liberal Prime Minister, Louis St. Laurent, was cautious about the severity of the flooding and seemed slow to express concern. Campbell was also initially slow to commit money and was criticized for his lack of sympathy.

Under fire by the press and political opposition, St. Laurent and Stuart Garson, now the senior federal minister for Manitoba, visited the soggy provincial capital. St. Laurent was asked by a *Winnipeg Tribune* reporter what federal aid would be forthcoming for the "little man". He replied, "Directly, none," explaining that federal aid would be channelled through the provincial government to an independent commission appointed by both governments.

Indeed, so much aid was raised from governments and public subscriptions that the commission acquired a surplus, which was held in trust for further disasters. But the damage was done. St. Laurent's "directly none", taken out of context, was widely represented as indifference on the part of the prime minister. This, coupled with the initially cautious response by Campbell, eroded faith in the Liberals,

---

[4] Molgat, Ibid., p. 11.

[5] Molgat, Loc cit.

Archives of Manitoba

Premier Campbell at the opening of Highway 10 in 1951.

marking the beginning of the decline of support in Manitoba for the St. Laurent government, for Campbell, and for the Liberal Party.

Just as flood conditions in Manitoba neared their peak, fire destroyed a large part of the city of Rimouski, Québec. Federal response was immediate. The next day, St. Laurent announced that in Rimouski, as in Manitoba, federal action would depend on whether or not there was a request for aid from the provincial government. Critics in Parliament and in Manitoba accused St. Laurent of responding with more alacrity to the disaster in Québec. Two days later, when another fire destroyed most of the town of Cabano, Québec, a similar statement regarding federal aid strengthened the impression in Manitoba that Québec was being favoured.

"In both provinces, the financial assistance given by the Government of Canada was exceedingly generous, but a more promptly forthcoming attitude to the Manitoba flood would have been politically expedient." [6]

Years after he left office, Campbell mused to a Liberal friend

---

[6] J.W. Pickersgill, *Seeing Canada Whole*, (FitzHenry and Whiteside, Markham, Ontario: 1994) pp. 349-350.

that he should have been more sympathetic to those who were flooded and that he should have provided more financial assistance.[7] He did, however, compensate future generations by providing the catalyst for a project that would protect the city from future disasters. In 1956, Campbell launched a Royal Commission on a cost-benefit analysis for building a dike around Winnipeg. The report laid the foundation for the Winnipeg Floodway, which was constructed under Premier Duff Roblin's watch.

IMPROVING DEMOCRACY

C AMPBELL WAS CONCERNED with fairness and democracy during his administration. As premier, he moved to provide the vote to all aboriginal people in Manitoba. He also provided for an independent commission to revise electoral boundaries every ten years, and to provide an elected speaker in the legislature. These were progressive measures at the time and the latter two led the way for similar reforms across Canada.

a) Redistribution:
In the years before Douglas Campbell, in Manitoba as in other provinces, there was a need to intermittently change the electoral boundaries as the population changed. Often, there was a temptation for governments to manipulate the results of the change in boundaries—or gerrymander—in order to have a political advantage. Campbell introduced a fair and independent commission to make the recommendations.

A bill in 1957 established a commission of officers appointed by position rather than by name. The chief justice of the Province of Manitoba, the president of the University of Manitoba and the chief electoral officer of Manitoba were delegated responsibility for fixing the boundaries of all provincial electoral districts in the province.

Two main problems needed to be addressed. First was the need to increase the representation in the legislature of the people living in Winnipeg. The second was to adjust the boundaries of the electoral districts so that the population of each district would be comparable.[8] As a result of the commission's work, the representation of Winnipeg was increased to twenty seats out of fifty-seven,

---

[7] Molgat, Ibid., p. 8.

[8] Molgat, Loc. cit..

and the boundaries of seats were adjusted so that each constituency was similar to the provincial average in population. The changes made by the first commission were passed into law in time for the election of 1958.[9] Since then, the Redistribution Act has been used every ten years to change the electoral boundaries in response to changes in population in Manitoba.[10]

b) Permanent Speaker:
In the spring of 1958, Mr. Campbell introduced two bills dealing with the position of the Speaker. Both were based on similar legislation passed by the House of Commons in the United Kingdom 125 years earlier. The first bill amended the Legislative Assembly Act to fix the salary and expenses of the Speaker, while the second amended the Treasury Act to make statutory provisions for the payment of the salary and expenses of the Speaker. Both bills received unanimous support.[11]

HEALTH CARE AND EDUCATION

IN HEALTH CARE, Campbell's government focused on implementing hospitalization coverage for Manitobans.

a) Hospitalization:
During the 1950s, increasing hospital costs were a pressing problem. Medical expenses were a growing burden for individuals needing care, but also for municipal councils and the provincial government, which incurred large bills for people who were unable to pay. A Hospital Rate Board was set up in 1955, to ascertain the actual cost of caring for a patient in each hospital. The government would then pay that hospital the amount per day set out by the board. A year later, the Government of Canada announced the establishment of a Hospitalization Programme, permitting the federal government to contribute approximately fifty per cent of hospitalization costs for the provinces, provided at least six provinces representing a majority of Canada's population agreed to implement the approach.[12]

The Campbell government decided to enter the plan, but

---

[9] Op. cit, p. 8.

[10] Loc. cit..

[11] Op. cit, p. 10.

[12] Op. cit, p. 9.

bargained for the inclusion of mental illness and tuberculosis. The federal government would not agree. Each month's delay resulted in a loss of $1 million in federal contributions. [13] Campbell decided to proceed. The bill to provide coverage for the costs of hospitalization in Manitoba passed through the House in record time and received unanimous approval. [14]

b) Primary and Secondary Education:
In 1956, the Campbell government passed legislation governing the negotiations between school trustees and teachers. The balance achieved by this legislation was so superior that it lasted for almost forty years without significant change. (The Conservatives finally amended the Public Schools Act to change the nature of negotiations in the mid-1990s, tilting the result in favour of the school trustees. The NDP wasted little time in amending the legislation in 2000, in favour of teachers.) Campbell also appointed the McFarlane Commission on education. It reported after the government retired and provided substantial input into the development of educational policies in Manitoba.

D.L. Campbell accepting an honorary degree from the University of Manitoba in 1957.

Manitoba Archives / I.6-c.1957

c) Post-secondary Education:
After 1945, there was a need to expand and upgrade the University of Manitoba to accommodate veterans who enrolled in university in great numbers after World War II and the Korean War. Short-term living quarters were made available and temporary teaching facilities were provided in the army buildings. The horticultural building was rebuilt to accommodate Home Economics, two brick barns were constructed to house Agriculture, and a judging pavilion was provided for the Animal Science department. The Medical building and the Arts buildings were also upgraded and kitchen and dining facilities were renovated in the student residences. New permanent buildings included a greenhouse for the Science

---

[13] Molgat, Ibid., p. 9.

[14] Loc. cit.

building; a new Engineering building at an approximate cost of $900,000; and a new Students' Union building at an approximate cost of $700,000. A new wing was built on the Medical Faculty buildings for a price tag of about $750,000, and a new Dental building, including equipment, cost about $2 million. A modern library allowed for consolidation of the major book collections.

All these changes enabled the Board of Governors to house the University, except the faculties of Medicine and Dentistry, on the Fort Garry campus. As well, the new dental building and increased staff funding provided for a Faculty of Dentistry in Manitoba for the first time.

GOVERNANCE, FINANCIAL MANAGEMENT AND BUSINESS INVESTMENT

THE CAMPBELL GOVERNMENT provided excellent management of provincial affairs, balancing the budget, leaving the province with no net debt, and engaging in restructuring of the management of hydroelectric power and provincial-municipal relations.

a) Finances:

In the worst years of the Depression, the budget [for Manitoba] averaged only $14 million and for a number of years both income and expenditures increased very slowly. However, by the time that Campbell took over from Garson as premier, the situation was changing rapidly. In the next ten years, the expenditures provided for in the annual operating budget increased from about $38 million to about $105 million, an increase that was more rapid, in relative terms, than at any other in the history of the province [up to that time].[15]

Campbell always aimed to keep the debt within manageable proportions and ensure that the government had reserve emergency funds. When he became premier in 1948, the province's gross debt was about $100 million and its net debt about $29 million. When Campbell retired from office, the gross debt was more than $200 million, but there was no net debt, because the reserves that had been accumulated were equal to the amount owed.[16]

---

[15] Molgat, Ibid., p. 14.

[16] Molgat, Loc.cit.

b) Creating a good environment for business investment:
Campbell and his government created an attractive environment
for business investment and economic growth by setting an example of sound fiscal management and by investing in infrastructure.
For example, following discovery of nickel in the north, a substantial outlay was made in the Thompson region by the International
Nickel Company of Canada (INCO). Under its agreement with the
province, the company agreed to spend approximately $175 million
in Thompson, to establish the business of the company in that area.
Capitalizing on the find and setting the conditions for the development were the results of careful planning and negotiation involving
many departments. Bud Jobin, Liberal MLA from The Pas constituency, and minister of Industry from 1956–1958, worked with
Campbell to fashion the future community of Thompson.

As H.C.F. Mockridge, a director of INCO, later noted,
"Campbell, he impressed me very much. He was sensible, reason-
able, very keen to have the project go ahead, but certainly not keen
enough to sell the Province out, so to speak. He was bound and
determined that it would be a sound and workable agreement in
which the Province as well as the company was protected." [17]

The exploration for oil in the southwestern region of
Manitoba was stimulated by the policies adopted by the Campbell
government. [18] Though companies in the province had begun
exploration as early as 1877, it wasn't until 1951 that the California
Standard Oil Company brought in the first commercial well, fourteen kilometres west of Virden. The Discovery Well was not only
the first producing well in the province, it was the first producing
well drilled in North America's productive Williston basin, which
covers Manitoba, Saskatchewan, Montana and both North and
South Dakota. Further drilling confirmed the existence of the
province's first major oil field, and by 1956, there were more than
700 wells in the Virden area.

RELATIONS BETWEEN THE PROVINCE AND MUNICIPALITIES

As FUNDS BECAME AVAILABLE the government increased aid to
the municipalities. This aid came in the form of increased uncon-
ditional grants to hospitals and welfare departments and assistance
with the cost of bridges and roads.

In 1951, a special committee on provincial-municipal relations

---

[17] Hugh Fraser, *The Great Thompson Nickel Discovery*, (Inco Ltd., Manitoba) p. 201.

[18] Molgat, Ibid, p. 14.

was appointed. The committee recommended the appointment of the Greater Winnipeg Investigating Commission to assess the problems of Metropolitan Winnipeg. The commission also reported after the government retired. [19]

Hydro Electric Reorganization

Before Campbell became premier, the Hogg Commission had been appointed to look at the future electrical energy needs of the province. Initially, the policy of the government involved the taking over of the Winnipeg Electric Company and the City of Winnipeg hydro plants on the Winnipeg River. [20]

L to R: I. Johnson, VP Border Power Cooperative, Minn.; H.S. Bliss, General Engineering Corp; Minister of Agriculture D.L. Campbell; Minister of Municipal Affairs W. Morton; Provincial Treasurer Stuart Garson; E. Schmidt, chairman of the Manitoba Electrification Enquiry Commission and R. Pearson, deputy provincial treasurer, 1941.

Archives of Manitoba / L.8-c.1941

---

[19] Molgat, Op. cit., p. 5.

[20] Molgat, Op. cit, p. 7.

In negotiations with the Winnipeg Electric Company and the City of Winnipeg, the government proposed that the development of electrical energy in the province should come under the mantle of the Manitoba Hydro-Electric Board. However, the City of Winnipeg Hydro Electric System would have control of the distribution of electrical energy in Greater Winnipeg. An agreement was reached with the Winnipeg Electric Company, which was purchased by the province, but the negotiations with the city were unsuccessful and the city continued to develop and distribute electrical energy within the city proper. [21]

The basic features of the government's policy on the development and distribution of electrical energy were set out in Chapter 29 of the Statutes of Manitoba 1949. Provision was made in that act for the appointment of the Manitoba Hydro-Electric Board and the general powers of the board were defined. [22]

The basic arrangement worked out by the Campbell government continued until 2002, when Manitoba Hydro took over Winnipeg Hydro. Under the Campbell Plan, the City of Winnipeg would have continued to control the distribution of electrical energy in Greater Winnipeg, while under the 2002 merger, Manitoba Hydro controls both the development and distribution of power within all of Manitoba.

Aware it would be necessary to spend large sums of money on the projects of the Manitoba Hydro-Electric Board, the province was increasingly concerned about its financial resources. Expenditures on rural electrification had already been large, but the financial policies of the government were built solidly around the Dominion-provincial tax rental agreements that had been made with the government of Canada. There was every reason to believe that tax rental agreements, with equalization as an important feature, would continue to be the foundation on which the financial policies of the provinces would rest. [23]

Campbell's government used federal equalization transfers to better deliver services throughout the province, as well as to expand economic potential.

Resources were used in part to expand critical infrastructure, such as the rural electrification program and highways.

---

[21] Molgat, "Campbell of Manitoba", p. 7

[22] Molgat, Loc. cit.

[23] Molgat, Loc. cit.

LIQUOR LEGISLATION

IN APRIL 1954, former Premier John Bracken, now living in Ottawa, received a surprise visit from Douglas Campbell. The Manitoba government had decided to establish a commission to enquire into the sale of liquor in the province and the cabinet wanted Bracken to be the chairman. The last major changes in liquor legislation had been made almost thirty years before by Bracken's own government. The Liquor Control Act of 1928 had provided for the sale of liquor by liquor stores on a cash and carry basis, as well as by home delivery, but had restricted public consumption to beer sold in rigidly segregated and aridly functional beer parlours. The legislation had been favourably received at the time and, in the main, had proven acceptable through to the end of the war. But as Campbell now explained, higher incomes, the greater availability of cars, and a change in social mores meant the legislation was being acknowledged more in the breach than in the observance.

In 1952, the Special Select Committee of the legislature made thirty-five recommendations for change in the provincial liquor laws. Action was taken to implement nineteen of the recommendations, but Campbell wanted the advice of the Bracken Commission before implementing the remainder. The commissioners began work on May 1954 with public hearings starting in July. The commission held twelve hearings at various locations around Manitoba. It also visited eight other provinces and six American states, and interviewed various noted international experts.

The commission's report provided a thorough analysis of the government's role in the field of liquor control. Throughout their deliberations the commissioners kept in mind that the state had two responsibilities: to provide effective control over the actions of individuals or groups when such actions were or might become anti-social, and to respect and protect the freedom of action of individuals or groups when such action was not contrary to the public welfare. The state, therefore, had an obligation to promulgate laws which would promote temperance in the use of alcoholic beverages since abuse in any form was against the common good. The state should provide for the adoption and strict enforcement of such laws, adhere to the practice of local option in municipalities and respect the stated wishes of the majority, promote by all possible means a sound and thorough alcohol education program, and finally, provide the best possible facilities for the prevention of alcoholism and the rehabilitation of alcoholics. [24]

[24] John Kendle, John *Bracken: A Political Biography*, pp. 242-4.

With this code in mind, the Bracken Commission recommended that the permit system be abolished and that mixed drinking be allowed in cocktail rooms, cabarets, dining areas in beverage rooms attached to restaurants, and with meals in restaurants. The commissioners advised the retention of beer parlours, as long as they offered light foods, soft drinks, fruit juice, and drinking water in addition to beer. They also advised the abolition of the old "resident" requirement, so that a purchaser would be able to take liquor to any bona fide residence. There were also detailed suggestions about hours of opening and the provisions of outlets in rural areas. The commissioner urged strict enforcement of the new legislation, including a stiff scientific test for persons suspected of driving while intoxicated, and a vigorous government-sponsored alcohol education program.

Bracken and his colleagues were emphatic that new outlets should only be provided if the majority in a municipality decided it wanted them. For Bracken, it was crucial to the success of the new program that democratic procedures be ensured and that local options be preserved. Finally, the report recommended that all beer, wine and liquor sales in Manitoba were to remain under the control of a liquor commission. [25]

The recommendations of the Bracken Commission were implemented in 1956. Voting in local plebiscites allowed, in most parts of Manitoba, for expanded sales of beer, wine and liquor. The ban on the sale of alcohol on Sundays was, however, continued until 2002.

THE END OF THE CAMPBELL GOVERNMENT

IN JUNE 1958, the Campbell government was narrowly defeated by Duff Roblin's Conservatives. The minority government of 1958 did not last long and another election was held in 1959. An April 30, 1959, a memo to candidates from J. F. O'Sullivan chairman of the Manitoba Liberal-Progressive Election Committee, provides an interesting perspective on the thinking within the Liberal Party.

> Without engaging in a competition of promises with our Tory friends, there are many talking points speakers can use to illustrate our approach, which has been summed up as 'Expanding Services in an Expanding Manitoba', without overtaxation.

---

[25] Kendle, Ibid., pp. 242-4.

The point, of course, is that services can be expanded without increase of taxation as the expanding economy brings increased revenue. It is reckless overspending —the inevitable consequence of reckless promising— that brings about tax increases and which will likely lead to sales tax, if the people give Roblin free rein.

Leading up to the provincial election of May 1959, Stuart Garson become involved and spoke in support of the provincial Liberals:

And through the years, we have always enjoyed prosperity and progress under Liberal Governments in Ottawa and at Winnipeg because their policies were sound and sensible ones.

They did not promise to increase government services and reduce taxes at the same time because they knew sensible people would not believe this sort of nonsense.

They knew that a government was much like a business or like a farm. If it was well run it would prosper. If it was badly run it would go in debt or go broke.

… Mr. Roblin belittles this Liberal Progressive Government that enjoyed the confidence of the electors of Manitoba for longer than any democratic government anywhere in the world. For on the record of delivering the good government at low cost it could not be beaten.

Mr. Roblin pours scorn on Mr. Campbell's conception of a little Manitoba. Was it a little Manitoba Government that negotiated the transaction and took the necessary positions to get the great Hudson's Bay Mining and Smelting Company enterprise going at Flin Flon and the large development of the International Nickel at Thompson and the Kelsey Dam? On the contrary, it was the demonstration of careful economical government administration, balanced budget and low interest costs and fair taxes that impress the executives of industries of that caliber. They do not fall for bally-hoo. You have to show real ability to inspire the confidence they have shown in the Campbell Government.

And so far from being careful in spending
the tax-payer's money the Conservative party, both in
Ottawa and Winnipeg, appears to believe in and practice greatly increased spending, greatly increased going
into debt, greatly increased interest and debt charges.

But the wave of support for Roblin was rolling on, and neither
Garson nor a good platform could stop him.

It brought an end to the Campbell government, though
he continued to lead the party until April 1961, when Mr. Gildas
Molgat, MLA for Ste. Rose, was elected to succeed him. Indeed, for
eight subsequent years, until 1969, D. L. Campbell was to sit with
Gildas Molgat as coach and advisor, as Molgat led the Liberal Party
in its role as Official Opposition.

Campbell's youngest daughter, Dwili, had not realized
that her father's primary profession was politics until after he had
won his first election as premier. Previously, when she needed to
fill out forms at school asking for her father's occupation, he had
instructed her to write in "farmer". The man from Portage la Prairie
who earned his living from the land, left a provincial legacy of
improved infrastructure, improved democracy, progress in health
care and education, business and employment. His government's
legislation to establish an independent Electoral Boundaries
Commission has since been copied by every province and by the
federal government. In a similar fashion, revisions to liquor laws
paved the way for changes in other provinces.

Campbell retired in 1969, but continued to be active, serving
on the boards of Manitoba Hydro, the Paraplegic Society of
Manitoba and the Portage Mutual Insurance Company, as well as
speaking to service clubs, senior citizens groups, and school classes.
His involvement with youth included the annual Douglas Lloyd
Campbell Public Speaking Award for high school students.

In 1988, he travelled to Russell to talk about the Meech Lake
Accord. Ron Clement, a local Liberal who chauffeured him to
Winnipeg said later, "I know he kept physically fit. As I was driving
away after dropping him off, I saw him through the window starting his exercises."

D. L. Campbell was a lifelong member of Assiniboine Lodge
#7 in Portage la Prairie, serving as Master in 1922. He was an
honorary member of St. John Lodge #4 in Winnipeg and the
"Honorary Past Grand Master of the Brand Lodge of the Masons
in 1975, who presented him with his seventy-five year bar at that

time. He was also a member of the Royal Order of Scotland." [26]
Gil Molgat, who frequently travelled with D. L. Campbell,
commented:

> In many trips through Manitoba I found that there
> was no town we went through, no meeting hall we
> entered, either then or now, where Mr. Campbell did
> not know any number of people. Driving through a
> town or village, Mr. Campbell would say, 'Let us stop
> and see—we've got time ...' and sure enough we
> would stop and chat with one or more of his many
> friends. Mr. Campbell always has time when a lesser
> man might ignore or forget his friend. [27]

Paul Edwards, leader of the Liberal Party in 1993, remembered the former premier saying to him, "Never trust the polls,
Paul. Politics is all about people." [28]

D. L. Campbell died on April 23, 1995, one month before his
100th birthday. His record of forty-seven consecutive years of service
as the MLA for Lakeside still stands as a Canadian and British
Commonwealth record.

---

[26] Tracey Thompson, *Winnipeg Free Press*, April 25, 1995.

[27] Molgat, 'Campbell of Manitoba', (Manuscript in Library of Manitoba Legislature), p. 3.

[28] *Winnipeg Sun*, April 25, 1995, p.2.

Courtesy of the Manitoba Liberal Party

Gildas Molgat c. 1961

7

Developing Big Ideas
1961–1975

Gil Molgat, Bobby Bend and Israel Asper

*"...[T]he Premier [Roblin] had ... clearly stated that the
sales tax in Manitoba was as dead as the dodo—and now
it's back in Manitoba in full life, flapping around the
province."* —Gildas Molgat

*"Everything is doable. If you're tenacious enough, you can
do whatever you set out to do. Because all you need is more
determination than the guys who are trying to stop you."*
—Israel Asper

ON THE EVENING OF SEPTEMBER 3ᴿᴰ, in the early days of World
War II, the British passenger ship *Athenia* was torpedoed and sunk
by a German U-boat. Among the civilians on board the 13,500-
tonne liner was twelve-year old Gildas Molgat. Molgat's survival of
that Atlantic crossing seemingly foreshadowed the drama of political life that would become his eventual destiny. Known to everyone
as "Gil", he replaced Douglas Campbell as Liberal leader in 1961,
and distinguished himself as one of the most gentlemanly politicians of his era.

Gildas Molgat began his primary education at Ste. Rose
School in Ste. Rose du Lac, Manitoba. An outstanding student, he
entered St. Paul's College (now part of the University of Manitoba),
and later enrolled in the University of Manitoba where he graduated as the Gold Medallist in 1947 with a Bachelor of Commerce
(Honours).

Molgat entered politics six years later, in 1953, as the MLA for the francophone riding of Ste. Rose. The newly-elected member was chosen to give the address in reply to the Speech from the Throne—a strong indication that he was considered to have a promising future. During his first year in the legislature he spoke on causes that were important to his constituency, including the need to assist farmers, especially young farmers; the problems of spring flooding; and the need for better drainage. In 1956, he supported a resolution in the legislature calling for the introduction of crop insurance on a federal and provincial basis. In due course, crop insurance was introduced, and it remains today one of the most important agricultural programs for farmers.

Though Molgat was never in the provincial cabinet, he was an active MLA who was re-elected in 1958 and again in 1959. When Douglas Campbell stepped down as Liberal leader, two men contested the vacant position: Stan Roberts, who had been first elected as an MLA in 1958, and Molgat. At the leadership convention of April 1961, Molgat received 475 votes compared to 279 for Roberts.

As Bernie Wolfe, who was there, said later, as a representative of the rural constituency of Ste. Rose and having worked for a Winnipeg financial firm, Molgat was deemed to have a better understanding of the province as a whole.

In 1962, Roberts resigned his provincial seat to contest, unsuccessfully, the riding of Provencher in the federal election. He went on to work for Pierre Trudeau, head the Canada West Foundation and later to work with Preston Manning in founding the Reform Party of Canada.

As the Liberal Party's first francophone leader, Molgat experienced equal measures of satisfaction and discontent. Though steady advances were made in the federal policy on bilingualism and in advancing the position of the French language, national Liberal policies to advance the use of French in Canada were also starting to generate some resentment in Manitoba.[1]

As opposition leader, Molgat was thorough and tenacious. He attacked the Conservatives, under Premier Duff Roblin, on many issues, including their lack of policy on sewage lagoons and their vacillations on the location of a wilderness park. (It was at one time to be on the east shore of Lake Winnipeg, then it appeared in northern Manitoba, south of Lynn Lake, before disappearing altogether). He also scathingly spoke of the failure of the Conservatives to address the huge exodus of young people from Manitoba.

---

[1]   Manitoba Legislature, Debates and Proceedings, 28th, Vol. 1, No. 1-67, p. 1420, p. 1428; 28th Vol. 3, No.

In 1967, Molgat began questioning the Conservative's multi-million dollar investment in a pulp and paper mill in northern Manitoba near The Pas, tabling "an extensive series of well-framed and cogent questions concerning the Manitoba Development Fund, CFI [Canadian Forest Industries] and Kasser."[2] Gradually, what was unearthed was the first major evidence of problems in what developed into the CFI scandal.

The genesis of the CFI boondoggle began with the Conservative government's launch of "Operation Industrial Breakthrough" —a campaign to build a huge pulp and paper complex in the north. After failing to attract interest from reputable Canadian companies, Premier Roblin and his government posted a worldwide advertisement that offered $100 million worth of incentives to private sector companies who could help deliver the project. A hundred million was a tempting offer, yet no traditional investors came forward. Eventually, the ad campaign attracted the interest of a Hungarian-American businessman named Dr. Alexander Kasser.

> Dr. Kasser was a shadowy figure who had put together large pulp and paper projects around the world and maintained a network of wealthy friends in Switzerland, Italy and Germany, but [in what should have been a tip-off] operated his North American headquarters out of a dingy walk-up office above a short-order restaurant in New Jersey.[3]

Despite this, the Conservatives were determined to proceed. A team of Manitoba officials, led by Roblin, travelled to Geneva to meet with Kasser, who showered his guests with the kind of lavish accommodation normally accorded visiting royalty. The delegation was well aware that the Liberals, under Douglas Campbell, had been instrumental in the development of the Inco Mine and the City of Thompson, and perhaps rivalry in the economic development arena allowed the Roblin team to be carried away by what they perceived to be a major Conservative coup. But they lacked the careful planning of Campbell, "unaware that Kasser was associated with a disastrous pulp mill in Sicily which at that very moment was devouring millions of dollars."[4]

[2] Duff Roblin, *Speaking for Myself*, (Great Plains Publications, Winnipeg, 1999) p. 137.

[3] William Neville, "Climate of Change" in *Manitoba: A History-Volume 3-Decades of Diversity*, (Great Plains Publications, Winnipeg), p. 90.

[4] Neville, Ibid., p. 90.

Instead of rejecting the financial proposal based on solid due diligence, they returned to Manitoba, jubilant in their belief that Dr. Alexander Kasser was a kind of modern day Rumpelstilskin, who could spin forests into gold.

As more details emerged after Liberal attacks in 1967, and a thorough investigation in 1970, the extent of the scandal and the loss to the province was clear. It was found that "$93 million of the province's money ... disappeared into a maze of 78 companies around the world. And at least $25 million of that was tucked into an untouchable Zurich bank account."[5]

But it was on the government's introduction of the provincial sales tax that Molgat was most relentless. It was clear that the Conservatives desperately needed increased revenues to accommodate their extensive expenditures, but Roblin had indicated in no uncertain terms that there would never be a sales tax under his premiership. When he abruptly changed his mind, Molgat pounced:

> Now judging from the way in which my telephone has been ringing since the 6th of February and the comments that one hears across the province, I think we could say that the 6th of February was in fact a very dark day in the minds of most Manitobans ... I'm told that there's a group of conservationists that have expressed some very definite interest in the sales tax coming in Manitoba, people like those for example concerned about the extinction of the Whooping Crane ... because it has been clearly shown that any type of bird or beast, no matter how extinct, can be brought back to life, because my honourable friend the Premier had ... clearly stated that the sales tax in Manitoba was as dead as the dodo—and now it's back in Manitoba in full life, flapping around the province.[6]

The Conservatives were caught unprepared for the onslaught of criticism. When queried by Molgat, the provincial treasurer (or finance minister) of the day, could not even indicate clearly whether the federal government would be paying provincial sales taxes in Manitoba.[7]

---

[5] Neville, Loc. cit.

[6] Manitoba Legislature, Debates and Proceedings, 28th, Vol. 1, No. 1-67, p. 956.

Roblin's poor management of economic development and the Churchill Forest Industries was a significant factor in the 1969 provincial election. Sadly for the Liberals, however, it was the New Democrats under Ed Schreyer who capitalized on the fiasco and formed the government. In early 1969, the Liberals had fought and lost four by-elections. The losses were a bitter blow to Molgat, who had toiled as leader for eight years, including campaigning through two provincial elections. Though the by-election losses were, in part, precipitated by federal policies, Molgat resigned as leader and decided not to run for re-election in 1969.

Recognizing that Molgat could continue to make an important contribution to public policy, Prime Minister Pierre Trudeau appointed him to the Senate in 1970. There, he served as a mentor to many aspiring politicians, including Jon Gerrard, when he was first elected a member of Parliament in 1993. In 1994, Molgat was appointed Speaker of the Senate, a position he held until 2001.

Molgat had a wry sense of humour and the common touch. He always kept in contact with people in Ste. Rose who knew, in Molgat, they had an ally who would pay attention to their concerns.

He was a great contributor to his community and served as a volunteer in many roles. In 1971, he was the founding chairman of the St. Boniface Hospital Research Foundation, created to help fund research and to attract leading physicians and clinical scientists to the hospital. Since its inception, the institution has grown in importance and stature, and is now an internationally renowned centre for cardiovascular science.

Molgat served with the Royal Winnipeg Rifles from 1946 to 1966, and became an Honorary Lieutenant Colonel in 1966, and an Honorary Colonel in 1985. He was active in the reserves throughout his career and maintained his interest in the Armed Forces right up to, and including, his later years in the Senate. He was the founding president of the Manitoba Army Cadet League in 1971, and served as the president of the Army Cadet League of Canada from 1977 to 1979.

Senator Molgat died suddenly and unexpectedly in 2001. His obituary in the *Winnipeg Free Press* captured the essence of the parliamentarian who had spent more than forty-five years in public life: "He was a man of great warmth and good humour, an eternal optimist with twinkling eyes. A man of simple pleasures, he loved smelly cheese, a good debate, exploring country roads (the rougher

---

[7] Manitoba Legislature, Debates and Proceedings, 28th, Vol. 3, No. 107–142, p. 2827.

the better), planting trees and outsmarting the beavers who dined on them. He loved people, and in particular the young, many of whose futures he helped shape." [8]

BOBBY BEND: 1969

Bobby Bend stepped into the provincial limelight after a decade away from politics. First elected in 1949, he had served as MLA for Rockwood from 1949 to 1959. In the battle to succeed Molgat as the leader of the Liberal Party, Bend's primary opposition came from Bernie Wolfe, an energetic city councillor. Bend represented the dominant rural wing of the party and Wolfe the city wing, which was increasing in importance. Others involved in the leadership race were Lloyd Henderson and Duncan Edmunds. Bend, an accomplished educator and a superb administrator, was chosen to lead the party, but he wasn't able to capture the need for new ideas and excitement in the election of 1969. The Manitoba Liberals lost badly and Bend himself was defeated.

The 1969 election was also a financial disaster for the Manitoba Liberal Party. The party's headquarters were mortgaged to pay for election expenses, and faced with the negative result of the campaign, it became impossible to pay off the debt. The building on Ellice Avenue had to be sold.

ISRAEL ASPER: 1970-1975

At the end of the day, you have to have mattered. You have to ask yourself did you make the world a better place than it was when you entered it, or did you just take up space?　　　　—Israel Asper

People were not sure whether he was a maverick or a messiah, but no one ignored Israel Asper. "Izzy" became Liberal leader on November 1, 1970. A man of incredible energy, he was far ahead of his time in his dynamic vision for Manitoba. Asper brought with him a "philosophy which blends a commitment to social progress with fiscal responsibility in achieving it." [9] He campaigned in an effort to bring economic prosperity to Manitoba and to create the conditions to make the province stand out among provinces in drawing visitors and attracting businesses. An expert tax lawyer,

---

[8]　*Winnipeg Free Press*, 2001 Obituary Notice.

[9]　Quotes are from a letter written by Izzy Asper in 1971.

Asper created a program that combined changes in both spending and taxing, and at the same time emphasized the rights of individuals and the well-being of citizens.

Born in Minnedosa and raised in both Minnedosa and Neepawa, Asper had the folksy charm of a country boy. His mother was trained as a concert pianist and, at age sixteen, had escaped Russian-controlled Ukraine by evading the rifle fire of border guards. His father was a violinist who studied at the Odessa Conservatory. Both his parents endured the destitution of the Depression and the intolerance and hardships of World War II. They found their way to Minnedosa and there they ran the local Lyric Theatre.

Israel saw himself as the black sheep of the family because

Courtesy of the Asper Family

Izzy Asper charming a crowd during the 1970 campaign.

of his non-conformity and his wry sense of humour. In 1956, he married his life-long partner, Babs, who supported him financially as he completed law school. He was called to the bar in 1957, and joined forces with his friend, Harold Buchwald, to create the law firm of Buchwald and Asper. He became one of Canada's foremost experts on taxation, and his book, *The Benson Iceberg*, was a bestseller.

There is no doubt that Asper's decision to enter politics

reflected a deep concern for the future of Manitoba. He called the West the "orphans of Confederation", and believed that changes politically and economically were needed at the federal level to realize equality. He travelled extensively throughout the province, holding public meetings and talking to students in dozens of high schools. As was said at the time, "The whole emphasis in the Asper program is on the individual—with all action directed to improving our quality of life, local and consumer rights, jobs and earnings, and government itself. The key to success is development—creation of new job opportunities and a broader tax base." [10]

On June 16, 1972, eighteen months after he took on the party's leadership, Asper was elected to the legislature as the MLA for Wolseley. It was a victory against rather long odds because the seat had been held by the former Conservative premier, Duff Roblin. Asper set up the first constituency office in Manitoba, knocked on every door in the riding five times and worked diligently to solve the problems of his constituents.

Asper's approach was systematic. He identified problems and had specific solutions. He questioned the province's economic climate and the role of government in the business of industry. His wide-ranging ideas included broad measures to change taxes and provide for more equity and rights for individuals. His bold vision included downtown redevelopment in Winnipeg, with an Avenue of Nations, ethnic shops and exhibitions, and a Cultural Heritage Park.

The platform he took into the election of 1973 balanced economic performance with social conscience. His ideas included an aggressive approach to make the province more tax competitive, combined with initiatives for strategically targeted spending in ways that would provide for a better social and economic climate for Manitobans. He introduced a denticare program for children, and an Institute of Child Care to create and expand programs, policies and ideas in the area of child care. The program provided for a senior citizens' income supplement. It included legislation providing for a Manitoba Bill of Rights, a strengthened Human Rights Commission and for legislation "establishing rules of disclosure of the investments and holdings, and the avoidance of conflict of interest by members of government, members of the Assembly, civil servants and government staff who have access to classified information." [11]

---

[10] "The First Ten Months", a brochure published in 1971 and available through the Archives of Manitoba.

[11] Ibid.

Asper recognized the need to overhaul the welfare system. "A man must have an incentive to work and produce if the economy is not to stagnate … Consideration was to be given to a guaranteed annual income program that would be operated by means of a negative income tax. Such a program would provide an incentive for people to work, replacing a host of existing welfare programs and eliminating the need for a means test." [12]

The 1973 election was hard-fought, with the highest voter turnout (seventy-eight per cent) since 1914. Richard Kroft (now a senator) and Peter Liba (lieutenant governor of Manitoba between 1999 and 2004) were heavily involved with the Liberal Party campaign. However, the media was not supportive of the bold Asper vision and when the dust of the election had cleared, only five ridings were Liberal red—Fort Rouge (Lloyd Axworthy); Assiniboia (Steve Patrick); Portage la Prairie (Gordon Johnston) and St. Boniface (Joseph Paul Marion), in addition to Asper's own riding, which he narrowly won. Initially undaunted, he soldiered on through the session of 1974.

The New Quarterback

Courtesy of The Winnipeg Free Press

By Peter Kuch, © Winnipeg Free Press, reprinted with permission.

From the moment Izzy Asper became leader, he was on the run.

[12] Manitoba Legislature, Debates and Proceedings, 30th, Vol. 21, No. 1-25, p. C1970-71 (MG14 D6) Manitoba Archives.

His reply to the throne speech that year was vintage Asper, characterizing the government's proposals as the "death rattle of reform in Manitoba". He attacked the government's inadequacies on several fronts.

I am bound to say that those of us who so eagerly awaited a declaration of what the government's new mandate would offer to Manitobans in the years ahead, or even in the months ahead, feel a sense of astonishment, frustration and overwhelming disappointment at the barren speech from the throne that we were tortured with. [13]

He continued:

What's particularly frightening is that if the abdication of responsibility to lead is so obvious and so evident from this, the first speech from the new administration, then Manitobans who expected much, much more have good reason to reconsider the choice they made in the election, for it is clear that the government has become smug and complacent in government, more concerned about finding ways to reward their political supporters than in launching new efforts on behalf of the people of Manitoba. [14]

Whatever happened to the Bill of Rights that Manitobans were promised in its first Throne Speech and again promised last year, and which on three occasions has been brought to this Chamber by the Liberal Party and on three occasions been refused support by government? [15]

Like his predecessor, Gil Molgat, he recognized the flood of students and qualified professionals who were leaving Manitoba because of a lack of opportunities. As the smaller communities

---

[13] Manitoba Legislature, Debates and Proceedings, 30th, Vol. 21, No. 1-25, p. C1970-71 (MG14 D6) Manitoba Archives.

[14] Manitoba Legislature, Debates and Proceedings, 30th, Vol. 21, No. 1-25, p. C1970-71 (MG14 D6) Manitoba Archives.

[15] "The First Ten Months".

shrank amid a huge wave of rural depopulation in the years after 1970, Asper condemned the approach taken by the NDP as largely empty rhetoric, and little meaningful action:

> What happened to the promise, Mr. Speaker, so eloquently pronounced by the Minister of Industry and Commerce in 1970, when he said words to the effect, 'We will see rural industrialization in Manitoba on a scale never before known'? [16]

He recognized that public sector spending was no substitute for private sector investment when he spoke of the failure of Manitoba to do as well as the rest of Canada. He reeled off statistics demonstrating that Manitoba was faring worse economically than other provinces:

> It now appears as we begin the second mandate of the NDP that there are going to be vast spending programs but few programs if any aimed at moving our economic output to the point where it can produce the tax revenues required ... If this government had simply had an economic policy which had allowed our province to achieve the national average, that's all, just the national average in annual growth over the past four years, our total production in this province would have been $800 million more, and because of this government's failure the loss in production terms to Manitoba is $2,600 per family. [17]

Asper attacked social as well as economic policy. He asked why the government had ignored their election promises of a denticare program and senior income supplement (The latter was a Liberal commitment that the NDP had taken for its own during the election but conveniently omitted from the throne speech.) Asper cut the NDP to shreds when it came to patronage:

> Whatever happened to the government's oft repeated pledge while it was in opposition, that it would end

---

[16] Manitoba Legislature, Debates and Proceedings, 30th, Vol. 21, No. 1–25, p. 64.

[17] Manitoba Legislature, Debates and Proceedings, 30th, Vol. 21, No. 1–25, p. 68.

political patronage and rampant pork barrel politics in the civil service? Mr. Speaker, how many more defeated NDP candidates and campaign workers will have to be appointed to the Boards, the Commissions, the Tribunals, the Agencies and the Civil Service of Manitoba, before this government's thirst for politicizing the civil service is quenched. [18]

In turn, environmental policy, hospital waiting lists, and opportunities and supports for northern Manitoba all came under the Asper microscope. Asper recognized clearly why the NDP government was so reluctant to improve environmental policy—because "environmental protection to the individual citizen means that the individual citizen will be able to stop or challenge government itself, and we saw last year to what lengths this government was prepared to go to prevent the individual citizen from having access to an attack on government policy." [19]

By not electing Asper as premier, Manitoba missed an incredible opportunity to move the province forward economically, socially and environmentally. Yet even loss was a stepping stone for Asper. He once told his son David, "you need in your life to lose really badly because only if you've lost and plummeted the depths of being a loser can you begin to appreciate even small success." [20]

But another career, in business, was calling. In 1975, Asper tendered his resignation as leader, and made these comments on his contributions to his Wolseley constituents: "For the first time, a permanent constituency office was established; the first riverbank park site was acquired and not a single highrise was allowed."

Asper remarked later, "my second career, that of being the Leader of the Liberal Party in the Manitoba Legislature, had fully drained my savings. Even back in those early 1970s, it was difficult to support a family on a salary of $14,000 per year. Man does not live on idealism alone." [21]

Forged from the missed opportunity in politics, and the recognition that he had to fight the media as well as his opponents, Asper entered the media business—in a big way. CanWest Global

---

[18] Manitoba Legislature, Debates and Proceedings, 30th, Vol. 21, No. 1–25, p. 64.

[19] Manitoba Legislature, Debates and Proceedings, 30th, Vol. 21, No. 1–25, p. 73.

[20] Allan Levine, *Winnipeg to the World—The Canwest Global Story—The First Twenty-Five Years,* (Canwest Global Communications Corp, 2002) p. 112.

[21] Susan Janz. *Winnipeg Tribune,* March 1, 1975.

began with establishing CKND TV Winnipeg and proliferated into a national and international media empire that included television stations, newspapers and the daily *National Post.*

Most important to Israel Asper was his much anticipated "fourth career", which he launched in 1997, when he resigned as CEO of CanWest to become executive chairman. The move allowed him to focus on what gave him the most satisfaction—giving back to his community. The Asper Foundation, created in 1983, was the vehicle for his philanthropy. The Asper School of Business at the University of Manitoba, the Lyric Theatre in Assiniboine Park, Canwest Global Park, home of the Goldeyes baseball team, the Manitoba Theatre for Young People at The Forks, and the Asper Research Institute at St. Boniface Hospital are a few of the many causes he supported.

The Canadian Museum of Human Rights in Winnipeg was his greatest project, and his family is dedicated and committed to making his dream a reality.

The community gave back to him, too. He received numerous awards including the B'nai Brith International Award of Merit in 1993 and Western Canadian Entrepreneur of the Year in 1996. He was inducted into the Canadian Broadcast Hall of Fame in 1995.

For a large part of his life, Asper and his wife pursued their love of jazz. Perhaps his passion for the genre is a reflection of his own character—inspiring, improvisational, creative, enlivening, unpredictable, but nevertheless with a clear target and an underlying vibrant structure. Israel 'Izzy' Asper died suddenly on October 7, 2003 at the age of seventy-one.

Many have asked why he left a reported $100,000 a year income in the tax-consulting field to take up a hazardous, strenuous and probably thankless task in politics. The answer was simple: "Fundamentally, I was so frustrated with the way things were going in the province politically that in order to live with myself I had to do something about the situation." [23]

Since the 1958 defeat, the Manitoba Liberal Party has made several attempts to rebuild. In some cases, the efforts proved to be ahead of their time and, in retrospect, Manitoba might have been well-served with a Liberal government. However, fortune did not smile on the party and the rebuilding continues.

---

[22] Levine, Ibid., p. xiii.

[23] *Manitoba Business Journal.* "New Liberal Leader Izzy Asper, Maverick or Messiah?" March 1971. In C1970-71 (MG14 D6) Archives of Manitoba.

Courtesy of the Liberal Party of Manitoba

Charles Huband c. 1975

8

The Coming
of the Lady in Red
1975–1993

Charles Huband, Lloyd Axworthy, Doug Laughlan and Sharon Carstairs

"This province needs healing. If the provincial Grits apply themselves to that job, they could pull the comeback of the century." [1]　　　—*Winnipeg Sun* editorial, 1984

CHARLES HUBAND: 1975-1978

A GRADUATE OF THE UNIVERSITY OF MANITOBA LAW SCHOOL, Charles Huband had served as a councillor for the City of Winnipeg from 1964 to 1968. He had been actively involved in the Liberal Party and after Izzy Asper stepped down, he was chosen Liberal leader in February 1975.

That same year, he contested a by-election in Crescentwood and was on the verge of victory when, days before the election, the federal Liberals antagonized Manitobans by increasing the federal gas tax. Though the final tally was very close (within 100 votes), when the polls closed, Huband did not have a seat in the legislature and the Liberal Party had lost its official party status, putting the party in dire straits.

In 1977, Huband was defeated again in Crescentwood in a general election, and in April 1978, he resigned the party leadership. Ten months later, in February 1979, he was appointed to the Manitoba Court of Appeal.

One of Huband's significant achievements was to push for

---

[1]　*Winnipeg Sun*, March 5, 1984, p. 10.

the purchase of a building on Roslyn Road for the party's new headquarters. For the first time since the debacle of 1969, the party owned a building to house its operations. The official opening of Campbell House (named after former Premier Douglas Campbell) was held in the fall of 1976. Precautions were taken, through the terms of its purchase and management, to ensure that it could never again be mortgaged to finance an election campaign.

During Huband's tenure, Reg Alcock became very active in the Liberal Party—working closely with the leader to recruit candidates. Alcock would go on to become the MLA for Osborne in 1988, serving for five years in the Manitoba Legislature. In 1993, he became the MP for Winnipeg South, where he made a significant mark at the federal level. When Paul Martin became prime minister in 2003, Alcock was appointed president of the Treasury Board and senior Manitoba minister.

Don Marks, later to become recognized for his films *Call Me Chief* and *Indian Time*, ran in the 1977 general election in Point Douglas. He managed an aggressive campaign, but fell short of victory. Nevertheless, his efforts were significant in heralding a Liberal concern for the inner city and the aboriginal people of Winnipeg. The election was also noteworthy because it marked the beginning of Meryle Dembinski's (now Meryle Lewis) career as a Liberal organizer. In that election, she served as campaign manager for Sue Jaravsky in Seven Oaks. Meryle has since run numerous campaigns—and continues to serve as mentor and guide to many Liberals, including the present leader, Jon Gerrard.

LLOYD AXWORTHY: 1978 and 1979

LLOYD AXWORTHY, a professor of urban studies at the University of Winnipeg, had a remarkable and distinguished political career that began at the provincial level with his trial by fire in the Manitoba Legislature. First elected as the MLA in Fort Rouge in 1973, and again as the only elected Liberal MLA in 1977, he provided valiant service to the party and to the Province of Manitoba. Between 1977 and 1979, he was the major public voice of the provincial Liberal Party, with his frequent pithy and cogent comments.

Axworthy was a consummate campaigner. He would once comment, "In my first four elections every newspaper called me to lose ... and I haven't lost yet. That says it all." [2]

---

[2] Tracey Thompson, *Winnipeg Sun*, April 25, 1995, p. 2.

He was perceptive and forward thinking, but was not without wit or clever disdain. His verbal attack on the throne speech of 1977 woke the chamber.

As I read the text in *Hansard* about [the Conservative MLA for Crescentwood's] description of the government's theory of government control being one of a little stimulus, a lot more neutrality, and a great deal of restraint, I thought that maybe he was for the first time really explaining to us where the economic theories of members opposite had been drawn from, which looks like it had been drawn from a planned parenthood manual, and that they had adopted really the rhythm method of government control as a way of doing it. I would only say, Mr. Speaker, that in looking at those remarks there was an awful lot more neutrality and restraint than there was stimulation. I would suggest that if they read those Planned Parenthood documents more carefully they'd find that the rhythm method itself leaves a lot to be desired. It's not very satisfying and oftentimes not very effective. [3]

He saw clearly that the Conservatives were, like the previous NDP government, "dedicated to outmoded propositions about the way the world should work."

He recognized an emerging alliance "between the reactionaries on the right and the reactionaries on the left." [4] This alliance would later come to full fruition between 1988 and 1990, when Gary Doer's NDP repeatedly supported Gary Filmon's Conservatives when the more progressive and forward thinking Liberals under Sharon Carstairs were the Official Opposition.

Axworthy stabbed Sterling Lyon's government in its Conservative heart by attacking on economic issues, criticizing their cut and slash tactics: "Are we suffering because there is a lack of revenue because we have been spending too much, or because there is a lack of revenue because we are not doing enough to stimulate the kind of growth and creative economic forces that we should be supplying?" [5]

---

[3]   Debates of the Manitoba Legislature, April 12, 1978.

[4]   Debates of the Manitoba Legislature, April 12, 1978.

[5]   Debates of the Manitoba Legislature, March 21, 1978.

He recognized the role of innovation in economic growth, and worried that Winnipeg was losing ground to Calgary and Edmonton.

> Where does the creative economic lifeblood come from? It comes from developing new products, new ideas, new technologies. How is this government going about doing it? Well, we are sort of cutting back all the programs on the provincial level that supply those, we have reduced the expenditures in the universities to the lowest annual increase of any province in this country and we now expect them to provide the creative stimulus. How creative can you be when you have cut back all your services, all your research, all your development? That's how you are going to create a new economic climate in the Province of Manitoba? By telling your most creative people, the productive people, that you are not interested in what they are doing anymore, that they are going to have to kind of go and do it on a shoestring? [6]

Axworthy held nothing back:

> I would suggest that the private sector that this government talks about is not really a private sector at all. They are not interested in stimulating the private sector, they are more interested in dismantling what the previous government did, They are more interested in engaging in a degree of vendetta. But if it really comes down to employing a full-scale strategy for the private sector, it is not here. I have not seen it, it's not available and I wait for it. [7]

He continued:

> The other test, of course, Mr. Speaker, is who wins and who loses in this Throne Speech Debate and this government action? Now we know who the losers are. They parade in front of this legislature ... almost

---

[6] Debates in the Manitoba Legislature, April 12, 1978.

[7] Op. cit.

Courtesy of the Liberal Party of Manitoba

Lloyd Axworthy, c. 1978

every day and I suppose one of the things we're going to have to do is work out some system of scheduling just to [allow] all the groups to know when exactly it's their turn to show up, students, tenants, women, day care people. You know, you name them, they were appearing. Why? Because they are afraid; they're afraid that there isn't the kind of interest or sympathy or sensitivity to the social concerns of this province and they have reason to fear, because there hasn't been any expression of confidence or support in these areas. [8]

As he closed, Axworthy accused Sterling Lyon's Conservatives of splitting Manitobans in two, leaving those less fortunate on the outside. He called them to account for harbouring the "spirit of the inquisition," looking for problems rather than new ideas and new solutions. And he pointed out that Manitoba was more in need of leadership which raised aspirations, rather than one which closed doors for many in the province. [9]

During his time in provincial politics, Axworthy, like Huband, involved many others in the Liberal cause. David Walker, who went on to become a member of Parliament for Winnipeg

[8] Op. cit.

[9] Op. cit.

North Centre from 1993–1997, became involved in Axworthy's campaigns. Joanne Purvis, who worked closely with Axworthy in the legislature, subsequently helped Reg Alcock get elected provincially and federally, and then admirably served those with disabilities in Manitoba.

In 1979, Axworthy went on to become the MP for Winnipeg Fort Garry and, after redistribution, for Winnipeg South-Centre. From 1980–84 and then again from 1993–2000, he was Manitoba's lead federal minister. From 1984–1993, he played an important role in opposition to Brian Mulroney's Conservatives. While serving as Minister of Foreign Affairs, he played a lead role in setting the human security agenda, in establishing the World Court, and in the effort which led to the International Treaty to Ban Land Mines.

Before entering provincial politics, Axworthy had been a member of the Manitoba Environmental Council, set up to provide critical input to the provincial government on environmental issues. (It was to be the start of a long tradition of environmental concern by the Liberal Party of Manitoba, which continued in the late 1980s when Harold Taylor was environment critic, and again after 1998 when Jon Gerrard became leader. Even the NDP recognized Liberal leadership on environmental issues by appointing Terry Duguid, a long time Liberal, as chair of the Clean Environment Commission in 2000.)

After a period with the Liu Institute in British Columbia, Lloyd Axworthy was selected as the new president of the University of Winnipeg in 2003.

Doug Laughlan: 1980–1982

In November 1980, Doug Laughlan was chosen Liberal leader after a stiff fight against Hugh Moran from Portage la Prairie. A year later, the Liberals failed to win a single seat in the provincial election, and in June of 1982, Laughlan resigned.

After 1982, the party slowly regrouped. It was a time of great divisions in the province and Jay Prober, a prominent lawyer, city councillor, and Liberal candidate in River Heights in the 1977 and 1981 elections, echoed the sentiments of many. "There's room in Manitoba for that voice of tolerance at the middle that Liberals represent." [10]

Critical to rejuvenating the party at the time were the

---

[10] Larry Krotz, *Globe and Mail*, October 14, 1982, p. 7.

Courtesy of the Liberal Party of Manitoba

Doug Laughlan, c. 1980

volunteer efforts of the "Gang of Eight", a group that included Doreen Froese, Hilaine Kroft, Meryle Lewis, Allison Molgat, Rae Scott, Shirley Walchuk, Diana Ryback and Berenice Sisler. Together, they eliminated the party's debt and set the stage for a move forward.

Sharon Carstairs: 1984–1993

THE 1981 ELECTION DID HAVE ONE LASTING IMPACT. Sharon Carstairs served as Beverly McCaffrey's office manager for the fight in Tuxedo, and for the first time, became fully involved in an election campaign in Manitoba.

Three years later, just when the Liberal leadership convention looked to be a ho-hum affair, the "Lady in Red" entered the race.

Long-time Liberal Bill Ridgeway appeared to have the early lead, gathering much of his support from rural Manitoba. Ridgeway lived in the heart of the constituency of Lakeside—which D. L. Campbell had represented for many years. A farmer and former union organizer, Ridgeway recognized the critical need for a Liberal approach to manage the economy to ensure job growth. His platform included a push to abolish the NDP's job destroying payroll tax.

Alan De Jardin of Winnipeg, and Stephen Zaretski, a councillor from the rural municipality of Franklin, were also on the ballot.

On the day of the vote for the leadership a *Winnipeg Sun* editorial pronounced, "the four hopefuls presenting themselves to today's delegates don't include any bone fide hotshots, stars, or charismatic leaders." [11] The paper's editors would soon be proven wrong.

Sharon Carstairs was an organizer, an orator and a great motivator of people. Originally from the Maritimes, she had lived in Alberta where she fought elections and ran in an election in Calgary. With the support of the party's youth wing, including young Liberals like Kerry Stirton and Nadim Khalidi, Carstairs won the leadership election on March 4, 1984. Her timing was splendid.

Carstairs came from a strong political heritage where dinner table conversation often included education and politics. Her father, the Liberal MLA for Halifax North, had served in numerous portfolios, including provincial minister of Industry and Trade. He briefly became premier of Nova Scotia in 1954 and was appointed to the Senate in 1955.

But it was Carstair's grandmother, Sophie LeBlanc Martel, who was a particular inspiration. Sophie and her husband Albert Martel lived with their twelve children in Arichat, Nova Scotia. Convinced that there was no future in the community for her off-spring, Sophie defied her husband and moved the children to Boston. When it was clear that his determined wife was not going to return to Nova Scotia, Albert packed his bags and joined the family. Sharon's mother, Vivian Alma Martel, was born in Boston and returned to Canada to marry Harold Connolly on New Year's Day 1935.

Carstairs obtained a Bachelor of Arts in Political Science and History at Dalhousie University, in Halifax, followed by a Masters of Arts in Teaching at Smith College in Northampton, Massachusetts in 1963. She spent more than fifteen years in class-rooms in Massachusetts, Alberta and Manitoba, in the public, private and Catholic school systems. While education allowed her to inspire children to maximize their potential, politics offered a wider scope for influencing change. She would later say, "I happen to believe that politics is the most important of all the callings, second perhaps to the church." [12]

In the provincial election of 1986, Carstairs ran in the River Heights constituency. The chances of a successful Liberal comeback seemed unachievable, but she performed well in a leader's debate

---

[11] *Winnipeg Sun*, March 4, 1984, p. 14.

[12] *Winnipeg Free Press*, February 21, 1986, p. 15.

with Gary Filmon and Howard Pawley, won her own seat in River Heights, and doubled the party's popular vote. Liberal candidates took second place in two other ridings: Jim Carr in Tuxedo and Georges Bohemier in St. Boniface.

Carstairs spent the next two years rebuilding the party's image and crafting her comments to receive positive press. When she entered the debate on natural gas supplies for Manitoba, the *Winnipeg Sun* reported, "We welcome Carstairs' entry into the energy debate in the hope that Manitobans might get some more practical solutions to replace the short-sighted responses of ICG, the Tories and the NDP." [13] She travelled throughout the province to gather support and to recruit excellent candidates like Scott Gray in The Pas, and Lois Feldsted in Brandon. As Jim Carr said, "Sharon Carstairs knew that the only way to rebuild the party was to visit every hamlet in the province, to take her message to crowds as small as one, to organize street by street, until the opportunity came for the giant leap forward ... Most of what a politician does carries no glamour, rarely produces immediate results, fetches few thank-yous and throws a huge wrench into the works of a family. The sacrifices are great, but without a strong foundation, nothing can be built." [14]

Carstairs was also an inclusive leader, welcoming into the party those who had come to Manitoba from around the world. Newly-recruited Liberals like Dr. Gulzar Cheema, Dr. Rey Pagtakhan, Errol Lewis, Wade Williams and Cecil and Patsy Grant, would make major contributions to the party and the province.

When the NDP government fell unexpectedly in March 1988, the Liberals were ready. At the beginning of the year, a poll showed the Tories far ahead with 50.5 per cent of decided voter support, the NDP second at 25.4 per cent and the Liberals third at twenty-two per cent. By February, Tory and NDP support were both down and Liberal support had increased. The fortunate timing of the Liberal Party convention, early Liberal advertising, and large and boisterous rallies kept the Liberal momentum building.

Journalist Gerald Flood described the scene:

> She [Sharon Carstairs] did the polka at the party's convention, then waltzed through the week that followed without stepping on any toes. And Liberal

---

[13] *Winnipeg Sun*, September 30, 1987, p. 12.

[14] Jim Carr, *Winnipeg Free Press*, September 30, 1995, p. A10.

Sharon Carstairs with Jim Carr, centre, and Reg Alcock.

Leader Sharon Carstairs never missed a beat ... Liberal advertising was the first to hit the small screen last week, and as of Friday, yard signs were rolling off the presses. 'It's been a wild week, exhilarating,' Liberal media co-ordinator Peter Johnston said. 'The reaction we get on the street is like Carstairsmania.'[15]

By March, a poll of all voters had the Tories at twenty-nine per cent, Liberals twenty-three per cent, the NDP at nine per cent, with thirty-nine per cent undecided.

Liberal policies resonated with people and with the times. Carstairs promised to eliminate the abhorrent payroll tax and to restore trust in government. "She said a Liberal government would turn alienation into trust by introducing legislation prohibiting permanent political appointments to the civil service, creating a provincial auditor with teeth, and preventing the awarding of government contracts to 'cronies.'" The message was well received.

---

[15] Gerald Flood, *Winnipeg Free Press*, March 20, 1988.

Indeed, the euphoria of growing Liberal support led to a *Free Press* editorial that stated: "The prospect of a truly Liberal government is one that should please Manitobans who have suffered too much from spitefully polarized politics." [16]

On April 26th, the Liberals rode the wave of support to become the Official Opposition, with twenty MLAs. Carstairs was the first female Leader of the Official Opposition in a Canadian Legislative Assembly. Jasper McKee came within a whisker of unseating the new premier, Gary Filmon in Tuxedo. Carstairs' win was celebrated by commentators who noted it was a "refreshing breeze that came from a busy mouth and an active brain." [17] "She was the fresh rose between the thorns of the NDP and the Tories." [18]

The Liberals elected in 1988 included a number of stars. Dr. Gulzar Cheema, the first Indo-Canadian elected to the Manitoba Legislature, became the party's very effective health critic. Later in life, he would go on to be the minister responsible for mental health in the B.C. Liberal government under Premier Gordon Campbell. John Angus, elected as MLA in St. Norbert, went on to have a successful career as a city councillor. Jim Carr, a talented speaker and writer, would have a distinguished career in journalism and then become the chief executive officer of the Manitoba Business Council. Dr. Al Paterson would continue for many years to have a leadership role in the provincial Liberal Party.

The legislative sessions after the 1988 election and before the 1990 election, were to be full of curious games. The NDP, badly hurt by the resurgent Liberals, spent much of its time attacking the Liberals and supporting and voting with the Tories. This Tory-NDP odd couple would become a source of humour as jokes circulated about the "two Garys" who were united in their goal of crushing the Liberal Party. There was more than a grain of truth in the joke.

One of the more curious NDP policy contortions came on the issue of final offer selection. The NDP, under Premier Howard Pawley, had introduced a badly flawed approach to resolve labour disputes that often tipped the balance in favour of organized labour. It was abhorred by Manitoba business, and Filmon and the Conservatives moved to abolish the legislation. A more productive Liberal amendment sought to provide fairness and balance in final offer

---

[16] *Winnipeg Free Press*, April 22, 1988, p. 6.

[17] *Winnipeg Free Press*, October 20, 1996, p. B2.

[18] Donald Benham, *Winnipeg Sun*, August 25, 1991, p. 14.

selection, and turn a poorly executed idea into one that was acceptable to many in both the labour and business communities. But rather than support a more equitable Liberal approach to resolving labour disputes, the NDP, including former union leader Gary Doer, voted with the Conservatives, revealing just how easily the NDP would put opportunism ahead of good public policy. Final offer selection, of which the NDP had been so approving only months before, was eliminated.

But it was the tumultuous debate over the Meech Lake Accord that was to dominate much of the two-year period from 1988 to 1990. Carstairs' principled opposition to Meech Lake was clear and was an important factor in her rise in status and the rise in status of the Manitoba Liberal Party. (In the end, when the Meech Lake accord went down to defeat in Manitoba, it took just one vote, that of Elijah Harper, the NDP MLA for Rupertsland, who stood alone in opposition.)

During her time as leader, Sharon Carstairs helped give definition to the Manitoba Liberals. She put it plainly: "We have to make it clear that we are a party that believes in free enterprise. But we also have to make it clear that we are a party of a social conscience."[19] The 1988 campaign captured the essence of the Liberal position with its slogan: 'Competence with Heart'.

Carstairs was a tireless advocate for better education for children, and for visible minorities that made up more than a third of Manitoba's population. She brought to the table a strong platform which emphasized improving social services through reform. She advocated changes in health care, education and training. She emphasized innovation and research as key investments in the new economy, and encouraged the support of home-grown Manitoba businesses in reaching out and competing in world markets. Her platform also included removing the anti-growth payroll tax which had resulted in job loss in the province. From June 1989 to June 1990, Manitoba had lost 12,000 manufacturing jobs, and 17,000 people had left Manitoba seeking work in other provinces. As Carstairs pointed out:

Bankruptcy rates are soaring ever higher at a record breaking pace. In the last ten years under consecutive Tory and NDP governments, Manitoba's job creation rate ran at only half the national rate. Manufacturing

---

[19] W.K. Williams, *Winnipeg Sun*, December 2, 1992, p. 13.

shipments were 25 percent below the national average. Retail sales growth was 12 percent behind the rest of the country. Manitoba had the second fewest housing starts in Canada.[20]

Carstairs continued to emphasize her concerns with the situation in Manitoba:

The government's recent fourth quarter financial statement indicated that provincial revenues are down, signalling that we may be on the verge of a recession. Declining revenues means there is less money available for our health and social programs. We have already seen the back door cutbacks to our health care system under the Conservatives to the tune of $66 million over two years.[21]

In retrospect, Carstairs' concern about an impending recession was accurate. Yet, when the Conservatives called an election in August 1990, they avoided discussion of the economy, instead running a series of 'feel good' ads featuring the premier paddling a canoe down a river or strolling along a beach. Carstairs called it the Conservative's "don't worry, be happy" campaign. She emphasized that "Manitobans can choose between a Conservative Party that has failed to get the economy on track or a Liberal Party that has the ideas and vision to take this province to new heights. Only the Liberals have a plan to revitalize the economy in partnership with the people of Manitoba."[22]

Carstairs promoted the idea that efficiency and accountability in government were needed to build the provincial economy. The Liberals proposed to strengthen the role of the provincial auditor and make publicly funded organizations like The Forks and North Portage Development Corporation more accountable through direct reporting to committees of the legislature.

The Liberal approach also emphasized the need to make government appointments based on merit, rather than party stripe, and the establishment of a clear legislative process to screen candidates

---

[20] Sharon Carstairs, *Winnipeg Free Press,* September 9, 1990, p. 7

[21] Sharon Carstairs, Ibid.

[22] Sharon Carstairs, Op. cit.

before they became chairs of important government boards and committees.

As Carstairs put it, "The new reality is that economic engines are fuelled by a complex set of factors. One of these is how government manages itself. It is our objective to open government actions to scrutiny, to depoliticize management of government to streamline costs and maximize efficiency." [23]

Despite all her efforts to convince voters that a Liberal approach was the best approach for Manitoba, the shadow of the outcome of the Meech Lake Accord hung over the Liberal Party and the tumultuous legislative sessions between 1988 and 1990 had taken a toll. The magic of 1988 was gone; the party dropped from twenty-one seats (having gained one when Gilles Roch moved from the Conservatives to the Liberals) to seven.

As Frances Russell said at the time, "The razor's edge margin and geographic demarcation of party support shows the huge odds a brokerage party like the Liberals faces to depolarize a province cleaved into two ethnic-class solitudes." [24] Carstairs had made a valiant attempt to depolarize the province but her attempt had fallen short. Yet looking ahead, her efforts may have set the stage for a future Liberal government to cross these solitudes and heal the deep divisions in the province.

Perhaps the saddest part of the 1990 election results was the loss of female Liberal MLAs Iva Yeo, Gwen Charles and Avis Gray, leaving Carstairs as the only woman elected to the Liberal caucus.

With the sharp decrease in Liberal numbers, Carstairs decided to leave politics after the 1990 election, but stayed on until 1993 to allow a new leader to be elected. She did not go quietly. In 1992, she chaired the "NO" side in Manitoba during the debate leading up to the national referendum on the Charlottetown Accord. She made it clear she was not following the federal Liberals, and that she was giving freedom of choice to members of her caucus. "I'm not a trained seal and I don't expect my members to be," she said. [25] Her fight, with most of the political leadership of the country on the other side, was successful, and contrary to the opinion of many, when the accord was rejected, Canada did not fall apart.

When she announced she was stepping down as Liberal leader, George Stephenson of the *Winnipeg Sun*, wrote:

---

[23] Sharon Carstairs, Ibid, p.7.

[24] Frances Russell, *Winnipeg Free Press*, September 15, 1990, p. 19.

[25] Riva Harrison, *Winnipeg Sun*, September 17, 1992, p. 12.

She has never lived up to the expectations many of us have for the people we elect. The politicians may not like it, but we do expect them to be deceptive, cunning, duplicitous and, when it suits them, dishonest. Carstairs was never particularly adept at any of those things. As her leadership of a provincial party passes into history, I think it can be said she was honest. [26]

When she opposed the Meech Lake constitutional accord, she did so because she didn't believe it was good for Manitoba. When she finally agreed to it, she honestly felt the country would break apart unless everyone supported it. Afterwards when she had personal problems, she was honest and talked about it, leading to an avalanche of negative stories questioning her ability to lead the party or even be a part of the political process. [27]

Even in early 1993, when many saw her as a "lame duck", it was Carstairs who emerged as the most effective opponent of the Filmon cuts to social services. Carstairs spoke with passion about the long-term social and economic costs to families. And even when she formally handed over the leadership, she vowed to continue to fight for the rights of children.

Named to the Senate in 1994, she continued to provide honest and forthright opinions on a number of issues, particularly when she took on the role (and the cabinet position) as Senate majority leader. These included the increasingly crucial issue of palliative care, which prompted major improvements across Canada.

Sharon Carstairs' story has been told at length in her autobiography, *Not One of the Boys*. She describes in vivid detail her time as leader of the Liberal Party in Manitoba—a party which is "idealistic, caring and prepared to stand up and be counted." [28] She also clearly stated her concerns about the dwindling participation of women in political life in *Dancing Backwards: A Social History of Canadian Women in Politics*, a sweeping history she co-authored with Tim Higgins.

---

[26] George Stephenson, *Winnipeg Sun*, November 6, 1992, p 5.

[27] George Stephenson, Ibid, p. 5.

[28] Sharon Carstairs, *Not One of the Boys*, (McMillan, Toronto, 1993) p. 62.

For some she will be remembered as The Lady In Red, not only because of her trademark use of the colour in her clothing, but as a public sign of her Liberal identity. For others, she will stand out as a woman of action, a champion of justice and equality.

She will be remembered for her uncompromising stands on employment equity, quality education, multiculturalism and the politics of inclusion. She will be remembered for opening up the doors of the Liberal party so that it now reflects the society in which it operates. Blacks and other minorities in particular, and Manitobans and Canadians in general, will sadly miss this great woman politician, who remained human throughout her career trademarked with the words— 'Conviction with Heart'. [29]

From left: Israel Asper, D. L. Campbell, Charles Huband, Sharon Carstairs, Paul Edwards, Gil Molgat and Bobby Bend, c. 1993.

[29] W. K. Williams, *Winnipeg Sun*, December 2, 1992, p. 13.

Courtesy of the Liberal Party of Manitoba

Paul Edwards c. 1993

9

Youth and Charisma

1993–1999

Paul Edwards, Ginny Hasselfield
and Neil Gaudry

*"If you teach violence, you get violence. If you run a mili-
taristic camp where the fundamental relationship is one
of abuse and disrespect, that is what you get."*
—Paul Edwards,
Liberal Leader, 1993–1996

IN THE WEEKS BEFORE the 1993 provincial Liberal convention,
Lloyd Axworthy noted, "We've got a situation where the Tories'
strategy is cut, slash, burn and hack, which is not creating jobs, and
the NDP is stale." [1] Opportunity was knocking at the Liberal door.

Paul Edwards was there to open it. On June 5, that year, the
young lawyer with charm and a gift for words, was elected party
leader. In his nomination speech he emphasized, "The politics of
division, the politics of business and labour, of north and south,
of us and them, must be replaced by the politics of 'we.'" [2] Edwards,
the charismatic champion of a new approach to bring people
together, had the opportunity to establish himself in the legislature and to further articulate his vision.

His 1994 comments on the throne speech indicated the
direction he wanted to take the province. He recognized, as had
Axworthy before him, that the world had changed and that the
approach of the Conservatives was just as outdated as that of the
NDP. He described how the Filmon approach provided a poor

---

[1] Donald Campbell, *Winnipeg Free Press*, June 6, 1993, p. A9.

[2] Frances Russell, *Winnipeg Free Press*, June 9, 1993, p. A7.

framework for economic growth, and that consistently, year after year, Manitoba's economy had done badly:

> In terms of gross domestic product—the Filmon government predicted 3.5 per cent growth in 1989; we got 1.1. They predicted 2 per cent growth in 1990; we got 1.6. They predicted minus 0.3 per cent growth in 1991, and we got minus 2.1. They predicted 2.4 per cent growth in 1992, and the estimate is 0.9 per cent. Madam Deputy Speaker, they predicted 2.7 per cent growth in 1993, and the estimate is 1.2 per cent. [3]

He documented the loss of approximately 16,000 jobs in Manitoba between 1990 and 1994, and the exodus of an average of 6,000 to 7,000 people a year from the province during the same period. "There is no greater tragedy," he said, "than the loss of those people." [4]

He recognized that the need for reform extended beyond economic policy. "It is time to take a new attitude in our province and make a commitment to the politics of co-operation, not division, the politics of inclusion not exclusion, the politics of pragmatic progress, not dogma." [5] He attacked the Conservatives' handling of health care and the environment and the fundamental disrespect the government had for many of its civil servants. He attacked the 'boot' camps for young offenders that the government indicated it was going to establish. He pointed out forcefully that when political leadership is focused on violent and abusive approaches to changing young people, those who receive this kind of treatment will grow, in their turn, to become violent and abusive. [6] And, in the International Year of the Family, he criticized the Conservatives' approach to families.

> Everything [the Conservatives] have done works against the family ... You slash education funding, you slash student social assistance, you slash Handi-Transit, you cut back the Family Violence Court, you

---

[3] Debates of the Manitoba Legislature, April 12, 1994.

[4] Op cit.

[5] Paul Edwards, *Winnipeg Free Press*, May 30, 1993, p. A7.

[6] Debates of the Manitoba Legislature, April 12, 1994.

cut back welfare. What family are they talking about?
The Conservative Family?[7]

In September 1993, the first test of Edwards' leadership came in a by-election in The Maples. Gary Kowalski, the Liberal candidate, trounced the opposition. Kowalski was well known locally and had been involved for years at the grassroots level; he campaigned forcefully, calling for "safer neighbourhoods and an end to youth related violence."[8] The by-election was an important test for Edwards, as well as Kowalski. Both passed with flying colours.

In March 1994, Edwards spoke to cheers at a Liberal convention in Brandon. "Our vision embraces hope and practicality and opportunity and this vision must not only be fiscally responsible but also socially acceptable,"[9] he said. He emphasized the need for the Liberal Party's plan to "rescue Manitoba from three decades of battles between 'two tired old parties'."[10]

After the by-election victory, Edwards travelled extensively around the province and recruited a superb team of candidates. At the beginning of the 1995 election, his vision for a prosperous province captured people's imaginations and he rode an initial wave of support. But, unfortunately, a series of misadventures in the early stages of the campaign eroded Liberal backing. As well, federal policies such as gun control legislation, slashes in transfer payments to the provinces, and cuts to the Crow rate covered provincial Liberals like a shroud. The party that initially had been neck and neck with the Tories and well ahead of the NDP, dropped in the polls. In the end, Edwards lost his seat in St. James constituency and resigned shortly after. Only Neil Gaudry, Gary Kowalski and Kevin Lamoureux were elected.

The results of the 1995 election were difficult for the Manitoba Liberals. They left the party one MLA short of having official party status, which meant a drastic decrease in the level of caucus funding though the legislature. The results also left a bitter after taste with many voters who felt pressured to vote Conservative to keep the Winnipeg Jets in Manitoba. It was difficult for the Liberals to accept losing when the government failed to keep the commitment that was at the heart of their election campaign.

---

[7] Debates of the Manitoba Legislature, April 12, 1994.

[8] Aldo Santin, *Winnipeg Free Press*, September 22, 1993, p. B2.

[9] Paul Samyn, *Winnipeg Free Press*, March 5, 1994, p. A9.

[10] Paul Samyn, Op cit..

Later, the Monnin Inquiry would reveal that a number of those close to the leadership of the Filmon Tories had also engaged in an illegal effort to buy the election and had covered their tracks with lies. [11]

While the immediate result of the 1995 election campaign was disappointing, one of the positive results was the many people Edwards brought into politics to run as Liberals. Many went on to serve at other levels—Anita Neville as a member of Parliament, Don Forfar as reeve in St. Andrews, Gord Steeves as a city councillor in Winnipeg, Elmer Keryluk as a councillor in St. Andrews, and Marinus Van Osch as president of the Manitoba Association of School Trustees. Bill Roth and Gail Watson, previously elected as reeve in Dufferin and school trustee in Winnipeg respectively, continued to contribute in these roles for years afterwards. Others went on to serve Manitobans in other ways—Art Miki as a well respected Citizenship Court judge, Joe Gallagher as a senior adviser to longtime MP Dr. Rey Pagtakhan, Val Thompson as president of the Manitoba Liberal Party in 2003, Dr. Walter Hoeppner as a physician in northern Manitoba, Clem Jones as president of the Rotary Club in The Pas, Linda Cantiveros as a leader in the Philippine community, Tim Ryan as a major organizer during the 1999 Pan American Games, Marilyn McKinnon as executive director of the Learning Disabilities Association of Manitoba, and Bobbi Ethier as president of Liberal Party of Canada (Manitoba) in 2003.

GINNY HASSELFIELD: 1996-1998

KEVIN LAMOUREUX was the underdog when he won election in Inkster constituency in 1988. He was the underdog when he ran and almost won against Paul Edwards for the party leadership in 1993. He was the underdog once again when he ran against Ginny Hasselfield in the October 1996 leadership convention. As he explained "All my life I have been an underdog and I don't mind that. Underdogs can surprise people." [12]

As an MLA in Inkster, Lamoureux was renowned for his work ethic. He was tenacious in the legislature, speaking on bills and always asking questions. At the end of his first eleven years as an MLA in 1999, he had missed only one day of the government's legislative sessions—when his father died. He had more than proved

---

[11] Doug Smith, *As Many Liars,* (Arbeiter Ring Publishing, Winnipeg, 2003) p 248.

[12] Paul Samyn, *Winnipeg Free Press,* September 29, 1996, p. B1.

Courtesy of the Liberal Party of Manitoba

Ginny Hasselfield c. 1996

his ability. Nevertheless, though the 1996 leadership race was a cliffhanger, Ginny Hasselfield won by a hair. Hasselfield was a teacher and an entrepreneur whose personality was a unique blend of style, charisma and a tremendous sensitivity to the needs of people from diverse ethnic backgrounds. She was born and raised in Deloraine, Manitoba, where her father was the local pharmacist, and her mother, trained as a nurse and an artist; devoted most of her efforts to raising her five children. After graduating with a B.A. in English and Political Science at the University of Manitoba, Hasselfield returned to Deloraine as a teacher, and later as the principal of the local high school.

She left teaching to become president of Cross Cultural Communication International Inc., a firm specializing in publishing, communications, consulting services and job training for immigrants. A tough-minded businesswoman, endowed with an abundance of energy, creativity and vision, Hasselfield was drawn to politics because she was frustrated by the actions of the Conservative government.

There was optimism in the air when she became Liberal leader on October 19, 1996. An editorial commented that, "Manitobans deserve better than a choice between a government preoccupied with settling scores with enemies and an Opposition party that is stuck in the 1970s. A revitalized Liberal party will provide Manitobans with another option." [13]

A second emphasized, "Now Ms. Hasselfield must show Manitobans that she understands the failures of Tory policy, that she is not bound by their privatization ideology or the 'don't

---

[13] *Winnipeg Free Press,* June 8, 1996.

change a thing' doctrine of the New Democrats."

Intimately familiar with conditions in rural Manitoba, and aware of the importance of embracing diversity, she was initially popular with provincial Liberals. Unfortunately, there was soon division and turmoil in the party—turmoil that led to her resignation at the end of 1997.

Neil Gaudry—Acting Liberal Leader: 1998

Neil Gaudry, the Liberal MLA for St. Boniface, became acting leader of the Liberal Party after Ginny Hasselfield's resignation. He served as leader until the fall 1998 convention.

First elected in 1988, Gaudry had a remarkable record of community involvement and achievement. He was fiercely dedicated to the people of St. Boniface, and to those in Manitoba's francophone and Métis communities. He was known as a tireless advocate on behalf of his constituents, and had the ability, even under difficult circumstances, to obtain justice and fair treatment for those who called for his help.

Born in St. Laurent, Manitoba, of Métis heritage, he had served several roles during Festival du Voyageur, Winnipeg's celebration of French-Canadian culture and the fur trade. Sadly, in early 1999, during the festival, he had a heart attack and died suddenly. It was a tragic loss for his family and friends, for the Liberal Party and for Manitoba.

Courtesy of the Liberal Party of Manitoba

Neil Gaudry

Banners in hand, delegates listen during the 1998 leadership race ....

10

The Building Continues

Jon Gerrard

By Gary Girard

Two CANDIDATES RAN in the provincial leadership convention that was called in October 1998—Jerry Fontaine and Jon Gerrard. Fontaine, Chief of the Sagkeeng First Nation for ten years, was well known. During the leadership campaign, he organized support around the province and demonstrated the formidable nature of aboriginal power in Manitoba. Gerrard, a physician and scientist who had served as member of Parliament for Portage-Interlake between 1993 and 1997, brought considerable cabinet experience, having served as minister for Science, Research and Development and minister Responsible for Western Economic Diversification. Gerrard won the closely fought race and became the provincial Liberal leader.

Gerrard's involvement in politics had begun years before, while he was studying economics at the University of Saskatchewan. Whenever possible, the focus of his studies was on the economics of running governments. Inspired by the strong economic nationalistic bent of the federal Liberals of the early 1960s and by Lester B. Pearson's activist approach to social and international issues, Gerrard became a young Liberal.

Almost immediately after joining the University Liberal Club, he discovered that the club was burdened by a significant debt. He determined to do something about it. Aided by club president Ron Rogers, he went about raising funds, then paid off the debts and had enough left over to take a group of young Liberals to a convention in Ottawa. It was to be only the first of several times that Gerrard would be involved in sorting out financial difficulties.

After completing his B. A. in 1967, he switched disciplines and universities to study medicine at McGill. In Montréal, as well as studying to become a doctor, he made use of his time to become reasonably fluent in French. He also visited various parts of Québec through his involvement with winter sports, bird watching and politics. A fervent Canadian nationalist, he was delighted to meet others who felt the same way, whether francophone or anglophone. At the same time, he was able to listen and learn from those who felt strongly about Québec and had differing views.

By chance, Gerrard was at the Québec City Liberal convention where René Levesque was ousted from the Liberal Party in the fall of 1967. The convention had been set on a Jewish holiday, and those who would normally have represented the McGill Liberal Club could not go, leaving the way open to a newcomer from Saskatchewan.

The following year, he skipped his medical classes to spend a week in Ottawa at the Liberal leadership convention, where Pierre Elliot Trudeau was elected leader. Though Gerrard had been working for John Turner, whom he felt had a better understanding of Western Canada, it was nevertheless an exciting time, and a good opportunity to meet people from across the country, as well as to discuss the nation's future.

In 1970, while learning "frontier" medicine during a medical elective in northern Newfoundland and Labrador, Gerrard met his future wife, Naomi. Both were working in a hospital in St. Anthony, Newfoundland, which was part of the Grenfell Mission. Naomi, a nurse originally from Pennsylvania, was doing a shift in the intensive care unit when they met. Two months later, she joined Jon and a number of others on a summer biological project studying bald eagles in northern Saskatchewan. After an international courtship during which Naomi worked in the United Kingdom and Switzerland, the two were married in the fall of 1972.

In 1971, while Naomi was in Europe, Jon finished his medical degree at McGill and moved to Minneapolis for an internship and residency in pediatrics. During his years in the United States, politics took a back seat to his medical training and, after his marriage, to starting a family. Naomi took a break from nursing when Pauline, Charles and Tom were born and branched out into painting, earning a degree in fine arts at the University of Minnesota. Jon completed his training in pediatrics, specializing in pediatric hematology-oncology (blood diseases and cancer in children), and became involved in medical research.

During their summers, however, and on weekends off, the

growing family continued its involvement with bald eagles. Jon and Naomi spent wonderful summers at Besnard Lake in northern Saskatchewan, banding, colour-marking and learning more about eagles. And each of the children grew up climbing trees and learning how to handle young eagles. In the process, much was learned of the birds, their migration and how they spent their time on their breeding territory.

From the start of his training in the U.S., Jon had always intended to return to Canada. By the late 1970s, he had reached the point where his research had gained international recognition and he was much in demand. Looking carefully at various opportunities in Canada, he was impressed with the research and clinical care being done at the Children's Hospital of Winnipeg.

In 1980, he was offered a position as a pediatrician at the Children's Hospital, and as an assistant professor at the University of Manitoba. He joined a team of people looking after children with blood problems and cancer and began a research program at the Manitoba Institute of Cell Biology on the second floor of the Manitoba Cancer Treatment and Research Foundation. With their three children, Naomi and Jon moved to a new house on the Assiniboine River, just west of Winnipeg near St. Francois Xavier. It would be their home for more than twenty years, until they moved into River Heights after Gerrard was elected as the constituency's MLA in 1999.

As part of his research with childhood blood problems and cancer, Gerrard built a research group that studied the inner workings of blood cells. His focus was on blood platelets, tiny cells—there are about a billion in a teaspoon of blood—that are important to the clotting of blood. The work was important and his reputation grew.

In 1985, when Dr. Agnes Bishop became head of the Department of Pediatrics, Gerrard was chosen to become the head of the Section of Hematology/Oncology within the department. The position was both as clinical head (for the Health Sciences Centre and the Manitoba Cancer Treatment and Research Foundation), and as head with respect to teaching and research with an appointment at the University of Manitoba. In this capacity, he led the provincial multidisciplinary team caring for children with cancer.

These were exciting years. With a team that included Dr. Nathan Kobrinsky, Gerrard's research led to a better understanding of bleeding disorders due to abnormalities in the function of blood platelets. Kobrinsky, working with Gerrard and other members of the team, developed a new way of treating children with these and other bleeding problems by using a drug called desmopression or DDAVP. They showed that the drug could reduce blood loss at the time of surgery. Kobrinsky also played a major role in introducing a new regime, called DOCTR, which proved more effective than previous approaches for treating acute myelogenous leukemia (AML) in children. Dr. Marlis Schroeder, another team member, led the effort to bring bone marrow transplantation to Winnipeg. All told, the Manitoba team, part of the North America-wide Children's Cancer Study Group (CCSG), was at the leading edge in the provision of care for children with cancer.

Gerrard was also busy with other commitments, serving on various boards and commissions. He chaired the B.Sc. Med. committee that involved medical students in summer research projects, and served as vice-president, medical for the Children's Hospital Research Foundation. By 1990, he had also become the responsible investigator for Manitoba for the CCSG. This North America-wide group of clinicians and researchers, all involved in efforts to improve the care of children with cancer, met at least twice a year to discuss the development and testing of new treatment approaches.

Throughout the 1980s, Jon and Naomi continued to spend time each summer at Besnard Lake with their children. There they monitored a population of some 100 bald eagles that regularly summered on the lake, climbing the nest trees to band as many of the young as they could. In 1988, their efforts led to the publication of a book from the Smithsonian Institute Press entitled *The Bald Eagle: Haunts and Habits of a Wilderness Monarch.* The book

The Gerrard family —far left, Jon; left, Pauline, and above, Charles and Naomi— banding young bald eagles at Besnard Lake.

Courtesy of the Gerrard family

was well received, and became an important reference work for anyone interested in these magnificent birds.

By any measure, the 1980s were productive years for the Gerrards. Jon was publishing numerous papers with new medical findings; by 1992, the total had reached more than 200. Naomi was actively painting and Pauline, Charles and Tom were rapidly growing up.

While Jon and Naomi had stayed out of politics while they lived in the United States, their return to Canada had brought politics back into their lives. Soon after his arrival in Manitoba, Jon joined the Liberal Party and in early 1984, he was asked to become the president for the federal riding of Lisgar. A few weeks later, on February 29th, Prime Minister Trudeau resigned. A whirlwind of activity followed, as John Turner, Jean Chrétien, Donald Johnson, John Roberts and Mark McGuigan competed for the votes of delegates at the federal leadership convention.

That spring there was also a provincial leadership race, and Sharon Carstairs took over as the new Manitoba Liberal leader. Like many busy people, Gerrard learned to ration his time. But he was able to meet each of the federal candidates and work with other members of his riding executive to arrange for Roberts and Johnson to visit the constituency. Each step provided further insight into the world of politics, as well as interaction with those who were political leaders in the province and the country.

In 1990, Gerrard was again involved in the federal leadership convention, this time as co-chair of Jean Chrétien's leadership campaign in Manitoba. Once again, it was a major learning experience that added to Gerrard's interest and involvement in politics.

Though Gerrard had been a Liberal since his days in university, and had attended various meetings and conventions over the years, he had never run for political office. In 1992, he began his quest as a candidate in a farm kitchen near Oakville, just east of Portage la Prairie. He was to find there were to be many, many more farm kitchens.

Indeed, he soon realized that his years growing up in Saskatchewan had prepared him for this. In many ways, his youth had been like that of many Canadian children, with outdoor trips as a cub or scout and involvement in sports of all kinds. He'd worked as a labourer on a sewage system and at a potash mine to earn money for university. But in one way, his upbringing had been different. For a number of years, he had accompanied famed ornithologist Stuart Houston all over rural Saskatchewan. Their focus then had been on banding owls and hawks, but it involved a lot of time in farm kitchens. Stuart advertised his interest in owls in *The Western Producer*, and farmers from all over Saskatchewan wrote back to say they had a owl nesting on their farm. Visiting the farms, Houston and Gerrard often stopped for coffee or tea in the kitchen before going out to band the owls.

Still, politics was a big change from trips to the countryside, which he loved, or working in a lab as a scientist, or looking after children as a physician. Many have asked Gerrard why he would give up a respectable career as a doctor and a scientist to become a politician. The answer is quite simple. He sees many things that need to change at the political level, and he is determined to do what he can.

For Dr. Gerrard, the journey from medicine to politics was rooted in events of the 1980s, when he was chosen to head the multi-disciplinary team looking after children with cancer in Manitoba. He found himself in an extraordinarily fortunate situation, for the team was focused on doing the best it possibly could for all children with cancer in Manitoba. The approach, which had developed during the 1970s and early 1980s under the leadership of Dr. Agnes Bishop, who worked closely with the director of the Manitoba Cancer Foundation Dr. Lyonel Israels, was one of integrated care. Team members included an occupational therapist and physiotherapist, a child-life worker, a teacher, a chaplain, a social worker and a data manager, and of course several doctors and an oncology nurse. Through the late '80s and into the 1990s with changes in treatment, the multidisciplinary team had been able to adapt to major changes in the nature of care for children with cancer. These changes included a dramatic shift toward more care in the clinic and at home, with hospital care reserved for critical times.

New approaches were constantly being introduced, but each new option was introduced as part of a research trial that compared the new option to the current best standard of care. Whenever new therapies were tried, they involved a careful evaluation of ethical issues, with informed consent being obtained from the child if he or she was old enough, or from the parents of young children.

Each trial also involved an honest assessment of the present therapy, comparing new ideas to existing practice, with efforts to ensure that tests or existing procedures were in fact really needed. There was a continuing effort to look at options with fewer blood or bone marrow tests or shorter courses of drugs to see if such approaches were as effective as more tests and longer treatments.

Not surprisingly, the effort involved in providing care in this setting was substantial. As the responsible investigator for Manitoba, Gerrard had to submit a large number of trials for local ethics approval and assessment. The participation in CCSG provided an assurance that protocols and practices used in Manitoba were equivalent to the best anywhere in North America. Most of the new ideas came from elsewhere, but some were initiated in Manitoba, as the team worked on making scientific contributions toward the best possible care for children with cancer.

And it was not always an easy field in which to work. While the

Courtesy of Jon Gerrard

Working to find solutions to childhood cancer involved Jon in many different activities, from intensive research to fundraising with companies like McDonald's.

dramatic improvements in treatment were making a big difference for many children, there were still those who died. These setbacks were offset in part by the team environment, which enabled close consultation and collaboration among the caregivers, and the multidisciplinary approach, which helped both the child's family and the community to understand the process. Members of the team, the teacher and the nurse in particular, visited schools attended by the children to help friends understand what was happening and to assist with the adjustment back into school. Caring for children at home meant working with the entire family, as the treatment of cancer involved a huge commitment of time, and sometimes cost, to the families. For many families, the social worker was critical to the overall success of the team in helping the child and the family.

"There were many moments of wonder as children recovered and were cured of their cancer. There were also moments of great sadness when a child's cancer returned, or worsened. Child after child, even when times were difficult, showed an amazing ability to smile as well as to cry," said Gerrard of this hard time.

Being a part of the team, and working for children were among the best moments of Gerrard's life. Even today, the faces of many of the children and their families come back quickly and it is a special joy when he meets one of his former patients, now grown up.

In the late 1980s, a novel drug was introduced, granulocyte-colony stimulating factor (G–CSF). The drug showed major promise in reducing the frequent and troubling infections of children with a rare disease called neutropenia. It also showed promise in helping children with cancer, so that they were less likely to develop infections. G–CSF was not immediately available in Manitoba. However, a group of parents, led by Winnipegger Lorna Stevens, saw the value of G–CSF and started the Neutropenia Support Association. Gerrard provided medical advice for the association. The parents provided information to other parents, raised funds to improve the research and knowledge of the drug, and took their case nationally by providing support to those in other provinces to get G–CSF approved across Canada.

Within a remarkably short period of time, their efforts were successful. The drug was approved and was soon making a major difference to treatment in Manitoba. Almost overnight, most children and adults with neutropenia showed dramatic improvement. G–CSF was expensive, but for many children it decreased the need for hospitalization, and thus reduced total care costs.

Through the actions of these parents, Gerrard saw first-hand the power of people to make a difference at a political level. Understanding the integrated team approach and its value in continuously improving the quality and affordability of health care also started Gerrard thinking about how it could be improved if that same approach was applied with a broader brush.

Time and again, in other areas of health care, Gerrard watched as inefficient programs were added and money was spent without rigorously testing whether the new approaches were effective. He watched as poorly applied resources resulted in care being given without adequately monitoring outcomes. In addition, resources were missing to provide the research and database underpinnings that were so critical to improving the quality and cost-effectiveness of health care being provided. Too often the needed teamwork and the needed integrated approach to prevention, research and treatment were not present.

For several years, his frustration at all this continued to

build. In 1992, after he had recruited and trained others like Dr. Sara Israels, Dr. Rochelle Yanofsky and Dr. Bonnie Cham, who could take over the job of looking after Manitoba's children with cancer, Gerrard decided to do something about the larger issues he felt were not being addressed. He decided to enter politics.

And so, in the fall of 1992, Gerrard sought and won the nomination to run as the Liberal candidate in Portage-Interlake. It was a heated contest with three others and was not decided until after the third ballot.

Jon Gerrard with Manitoba farmers near Brookdale, right, and below, with a fisherman on the Dauphin River.

Photos from the collection of Jon Gerrard

The riding of Portage-Interlake extended west from the Gerrard home to include Portage la Prairie and the surrounding area. To the north and east it stretched between Lake Winnipeg on the east and Lakes Manitoba and Winnipegosis on the west. It was a wonderful riding in the heart of Manitoba with a mix of grassroots people, farmers and fishermen living in small towns and larger communities like Gimli, Stonewall, Teulon, Arborg, Riverton, Fisher Branch, Ashern, Eriksdale, Lundar, St. Laurent and Elie.

For the next year, until the federal election of October 1993,

Gerrard's campaign gradually built momentum and on election day, voters chose to send him to Ottawa as their representative. The Monday after the election, he got a call to meet Prime Minister Jean Chrétien. He was to be in the cabinet as the Secretary of State for Science, Research and Development. On November 4th, the cabinet was sworn in, with John Manley as minister of Industry. Gerrard would work very closely with him at Industry Canada.

For Gerrard, it was an incredible opportunity. His first university degree, a B.A. in economics, together with his training in medicine and in science, enabled him to quickly grasp the material he was given. Gerrard was also familiar with technology and the internet, having worked in medical research. He was to learn a lot more in a short time.

In some ways, the position was ideal for Gerrard. He understood the internet and was determined to bring its benefits to rural parts of Canada. At the time, people in rural areas had to dial long distance in order to access the internet to make contact with others across the country or even in Winnipeg. He even knew someone with a $900 bill for just one month for long distance charges. This, he felt, had to be changed. And within a remarkably short period of time, Gerrard was able to get the information highway into the Throne Speech and onto the national agenda. On February 2, 1994, he spoke to the Information Technology Association of Canada to outline the goals and principles of the government's information highway strategy. Shortly afterwards, an Information Highway Advisory Council was in place and charged with making direct recommendations for action. Even more important, these recommendations were implemented as fast as they rolled out of the meetings. It was an exciting time.

Gerrard's position also included a role in promoting environmental industries. He was able to see first hand the opportunities and the needs in this area. Now his knowledge of environmental issues, garnered from years of work with eagles and his lifelong concern for the environment proved useful.

His riding of Portage-Interlake also occupied much of his time. It was comprised of some ninety communities, varying in size from tiny hamlets to the City of Portage la Prairie with about 13,000 people. In order to serve his constituents, he travelled extensively, looking for opportunities to help people and strengthen their communities. It was rewarding seeing old businesses expand and new ones develop and it was an opportunity to be part of major changes and improvements in the area. Gerrard loved what he was doing and the wonderful people he was working with—Sheila

Champagne, for example, was incredible. But many others con-tributed—among them Paulette Taplin, Ginette Jolin, Scott Turbett, Orville Woodford, Ryan Moran, Alan Green and Barbara Doan.

But not everything moved as quickly as the information highway agenda. In trying to change the national approach to science and technology, he was to find much difference of opinion as to what needed to be done. To gather support and build consensus to move forward, Gerrard led a series of consultations in Science and Technology at more than twenty centres across Canada. These were followed by regional and national meetings, with John Manley taking a major role.

The consultations went well, but the report ran into rough water with the tough budget of 1995. There were also divisions within the government, the result of differing opinions in the many departments that were involved in one way or another in science or technology. Nevertheless, the problems were gradually overcome, and over the next several years huge changes were made in the gov-ernment's approach to science and technology. These included the development of major programs like Technology Partnerships Canada and the Canadian Foundation for Innovation; increased funding for the various research granting councils; the change from the Medical Research Council to the Canadian Institutes for Health Research, and many others. Some of the programs, including the Canada Research Chairs, were not completed until after Gerrard left office, but the groundwork had been laid for change. By 2000, the changes were having a major impact; more scientists were returning to Canada to work, and many scientists living or training in Canada were better able to get positions here.

But not everything went smoothly. In some areas, Gerrard found as a novice politician he had much to learn. In his constit-uency, problems were emerging and the demands of his cabinet position meant he was less available to find solutions. A boundary commission recommended dividing Portage-Interlake in half, with the southeast half joining the area further south and east as Portage -Lisgar and the northeast half joining the Selkirk area to become Selkirk-Interlake. Living right on the boundary between the new constituencies, Gerrard felt as though his life was being torn in two. For a while, he found that people in both constituencies expected him to deal with their concerns. For a rookie MP with a cabinet responsibility, he was soon overextended. In the end, after much discussion and debate, he made the decision to run in Selkirk-Interlake in the coming election.

But there was another major issue. The 1993 Liberal Red

Book of campaign promises had made mention of strengthening gun control. In 1994, this jumped onto the national agenda as Justice Minister Alan Rock brought forward a recommendation to register all firearms. Handguns had been registered in Canada since the 1930s, but in 1994, that registry still operated primarily as a paper-based system. Clearly, it needed to be computerized, making the information quickly available to police officers to check the ownership of a particular handgun. Rock proposed to make this change, and at the same time include rifles and other long guns as well. There was an immediate outcry from long-gun owners across Canada. Nowhere was this louder than in the Interlake, one of Western Canada's prime hunting areas.

Gerrard knew it would be a tough issue and he did not handle it well. He believed that if all guns were to be registered, the process should be tested in one region or one province to make sure the system worked well and was effective in reducing crime, before it was introduced across the country. But this view was rejected. Instead, Alan Rock's efforts were like a steamroller moving across the country. Though there were loud disagreements in meeting after meeting at the national Liberal caucus, the steamroller kept moving on, supported by national polls that showed strong support from Canadians in urban areas.

Gerrard was moved by stories from both sides of the issue. On one side, one of his closest supporters was convinced that if the legislation had been in effect earlier, her parents would still be alive. The man who had shot her parents had borrowed the rifle he used from a neighbour. She was convinced that had the guns been registered, the neighbour would have been much less likely to lend his weapon. She was probably correct.

On the other side, opponents of the legislation brought forward studies from other jurisdictions showing that registration per se was less effective in reducing crime than had been suggested by proponents of the legislation.

In retrospect, Gerrard felt he should have made greater efforts to bring together the MPs from rural ridings in Western Canada and hammer home what he suspected: if the legislation was passed as proposed, it was likely that all Liberal seats in rural Western Canada would be lost for a decade. Gerrard and others in the Liberal caucus did suggest changes, and a few modest ones were made, but it was not enough. And in the years since, numerous problems, including major cost overruns, have plagued the registry, giving it an increasingly bad reputation. Nevertheless, since 1995, there has been a sharp decrease in crimes using firearms in Canada.

The jury may still be out on the final effectiveness, or lack of it, of this legislation.

For his part, when it came to a vote in the House of Commons, as a cabinet minister Gerrard had a choice of supporting the legislation or resigning. Deciding that he could do much more for the people of Portage-Interlake by staying in cabinet, he voted for the bill. As John Manley and he walked back to the ministerial offices on Queen Street after the vote, Gerrard shared his suspicion that the vote was likely to result in his defeat in the next election.

Despite this, Gerrard was determined to do everything he could for the people of Portage-Interlake while he was there. This was made easier in early 1996 when he was given responsibility for Western Economic Diversification as well as for Science, Research and Development.

For Manitoba, for those interested in rural development in rural Western Canada and for the people of Portage-Interlake, Gerrard's time in Western Economic Diversification was very productive. The local Community Futures Development Corporation network was extended to all of rural Western Canada. New opportunities were provided for youth entrepreneurs, for entrepreneurs with disabilities and for the use of technology to access business opportunities.

Gerrard also worked with the provinces to develop online and single window access to business services and hosted small business fairs to promote increased entrepreneurship and business development. The goal was to help aspiring entrepreneurs in starting and growing businesses. Gerrard travelled extensively throughout Western Canada during this period, trying to improve understanding of and involvement in entrepreneurship and attempting to produce a cultural change aimed at providing more emphasis on developing entrepreneurial skills.

Entrepreneurs, he believes, are the moving force behind both the creation of new jobs and improved economic opportunities, and the changes in the world are increasingly creating global opportunities, even for those living in rural areas.

In his responsibility for Western Economic Diversification, Gerrard also worked closely with Foreign Affairs Minister Lloyd Axworthy to ensure a smooth transition in the ownership of the rail line to the Port of Churchill from Canadian National to a short-line company. This was achieved when OmniTrax took over the rail line. To date the American company has run the line successfully, though not without challenges. Few realize today how close

Manitoba came to losing its rail line to Churchill. Gerrard saw it as part of building Manitoba, and building the economy of Western Canada.

His position with Western Economic Diversification opened other opportunities, including promoting advances in functional foods and nutraceuticals, and bringing natural gas to communities in the Interlake, but Gerrard was increasingly taken out of his constituency. A normal week meant two to three days in Ottawa, two to three days somewhere in the rest of Canada or the world, and two to three days in Manitoba. There was little time for rest, though he insisted on spending at least one day every two weeks with his family.

The election call came earlier than expected and in Manitoba it came with a complication. Called in late April for early June 1997, the campaign coincided with the threat of the Flood of the Century. For Gerrard, the timing could hardly have been worse. Indeed, it turned out to be an election from hell. Everything that could have gone wrong did. Accepting the blame, Gerrard acknowledges that many of the mistakes were his own. His wife Naomi and many others campaigned tirelessly, but on election night, he fell short by fifty-two votes. He had lost. He was out of politics.

It was a devastating blow. Jon and Naomi packed up their things in their condominium in Hull, which they had chosen because it was close to the Gatineau Hills and more affordable than Ottawa, and moved everything back to their home near St. Francois Xavier. Gerrard returned to the Children's Hospital in Winnipeg where, using his contacts and knowledge of the information highway, he helped with several initiatives aimed at developing improved internet access to health care both at the hospital and for children with disabilities and their families. He also assisted Dr. Henry Friesen in his efforts, nationally, with Alan Rock to complete the transformation of the Medical Research Council into a new Canadian Institutes for Health Research.

Then in January 1998, Manitoba Liberal Leader Ginny Hasselfield resigned. Until then, Gerrard had never seriously considered entering provincial politics. His goal had been to change things at the federal level. However, other Liberals wanted him to think about running provincially. Initially he was reluctant about these approaches, but he did begin examining the possibility.

In Ottawa, it had been clear to him on numerous occasions that change was needed at the provincial level in Manitoba. Compared to other provinces, governments in Manitoba had often not understood how to take advantage of national funding opportunities. Manitoba politicians tended to come begging for support from Ottawa, rather than recognizing that a large proportion of the funds from Ottawa must flow in a way that treats provinces fairly, with groups, individuals or businesses within provinces competing for federal dollars. Just as federal dollars flow to Olympic level athletes based on their performance, funding for research and many other areas depends on the province acting to provide a base that allows its citizens and its businesses to compete.

Nationally, we have moved from an age of entitlement to an age of excellence. Instead of begging, Manitoba needs to compete. This means making provincial investments in critical areas, and developing a base of businesses in new areas so that Manitoba can compete with other provinces. Gerrard came to appreciate that improving the situation in Manitoba could not be done just from Ottawa. Change also had to come at the provincial level.

In health care, with which Gerrard was very much concerned, it was particularly clear that changes were needed at the provincial level. Ottawa could do a great deal, but the hands-on management of health care was the responsibility of each province, and meaningful decisions had to be made at the provincial level. For some time, it had been apparent that major improvements were needed in the way health care was being managed in Manitoba. Perhaps getting involved in provincial politics would provide an opportunity to work for the changes needed.

From a personal perspective, Gerrard also knew that he had walked through the door from medical practice and scientific research into politics. Though he had come back to the Children's Hospital for a short while, he knew that it would be much more difficult for him to go back long term.

From February to June, he spent a lot of time talking with people about the Manitoba Liberal Party and considering the possibility of moving his focus to the provincial level. He knew if he made the move he could make use of what he had learned in Ottawa to improve how he would approach provincial politics. In particular, his battles had taught him about the power of governments. When an individual fights against an abuse by government, the contest is clearly unequal, and great care must be taken that the rights of citizens are not overlooked.

Considering his options, he also knew that the Manitoba Liberal Party had some wonderful people who had worked very hard and believed strongly in it. He knew, too, that there were many who had become disillusioned and disheartened by the lack of success. But the Manitoba Liberal Party surely was a party to be proud of, one that should recognize the hard work of leaders like Israel

(Izzy) Asper, Charles Huband, Sharon Carstairs, Paul Edwards and Ginny Hasselfield. He also looked carefully at the alternatives—the Conservatives under Gary Filmon and the NDP under Gary Doer. In both cases, he felt he could see where more could be done to achieve the prosperity he believed Manitoba deserved.

Jon with Jerry Fontaine, centre, and band members at Puktawagan.

Courtesy of the Liberal Party of Manitoba

Gerrard believed he knew what had to be done to move Manitoba forward. His experience in health care and government and his knowledge of economic and environmental issues allowed him to see a clear path. And though he looked for others who could take the party and the province forward, none had quite the qualifications that he believed were needed.

Chief Jerry Fontaine of the Sagkeeng First Nation had put his name forward to lead the party. Gerrard had a lot of respect for Chief Fontaine, who was well qualified in many ways, having served for ten years as chief. But after much deliberation, Gerrard decided to take the plunge and ran against him for the leadership. As indicated earlier, Gerrard became party leader.

The party he inherited, however, was disorganized and in debt. With the next provincial election less than a year away, it was not as prepared as it needed to be. Not all fifty-seven candidates got the signatures required for their names to be on the ballot and the party suffered negative publicity when it was not prepared for several issues that arose. The result was a perception that the party was not ready to govern and in 1999, Gerrard was the only Liberal elected.

After the election, he worked tirelessly to rebuild the party, travelling extensively across the province over the next four years. Slowly, the party was brought out of debt. He also met with many community groups, business and social organizations, and scientific communities, believing that the answers to many of the challenges facing Manitoba today do not lie with any one group or interest. He believes that Liberals can best serve Manitobans by maintaining a position in the centre of the political spectrum, and building on the best ideas.

In 2001, as a result of changes to the provincial election finances act, the provincial Liberal Party was forced to separate from its federal counterpart. The name was changed to the Manitoba Liberal Party, emphasizing the priority of putting Manitoba first. The party was restructured with a new board of directors and in 2003 moved into Molgat Place, its new headquarters on the corner of Broadway and Langside, where it shares space with the federal party. Located just a short distance from the Manitoba Legislature,

From the collection of Jon Gerrard

Jon Gerrard, right, with Allison Molgat and then Prime Minister Paul Martin at the opening of Molgat Place, September 23, 2004.

it has full disability access.

In the provincial election of 2003, the party demonstrated its organization and ideals. All fifty-seven candidates were ready. Twenty-three of them, or forty per cent, were women, a record in Canadian politics. There was also a remarkable mix of ethnic and cultural backgrounds, with seven aboriginal candidates, and representatives from the Caribbean, Ukrainian, Polish, Philippine and Indo-Canadian communities. The platform and fiscal plan were comprehensive and well conceived, and judged by many to be the best of the three parties. But without the financing needed to advertise and carry the message broadly to Manitobans, it was not possible to achieve a breakthrough to increase Liberal support.

Nor was the weather as co-operative as it might have been. May was beautiful and the long, warm evenings lured Manitobans outdoors where they found enjoying spring was preferable to watch the election debates unfold. Many also considered the election bland. The NDP had spent four years taking as little action as possible, and Gary Doer's government had not yet offended enough voters to give opposition parties a boost. The Conservatives were suffering from infighting and a lack of clear policies, due in part to having acclaimed a new leader who was largely unknown to voters. Stuart Murray had begun his tenure as leader by hiring Taras Sokolyk, who had been associated with the vote-rigging events of 1995. That this was done without informing the senior people in the party had upset many.

As a result, the Liberals fell short of the seats as needed to achieve full party status in the legislature. Jon Gerrard was re-elected and the party took a positive step forward with the election of Kevin Lamoureux in Inkster. He had served previously as the MLA from Inkster from 1988–1999 and his experience in the legislature brought Gerrard a skilled and experienced partner. It was solid progress.

So, while the results were not as good as was hoped, the party was growing once again, out of debt, with solid policies developed over several years, increasing membership and organization, and a solid leader. With the support of its members, the next forty years look to be much better than the last forty.

Two by-elections in June 2004 showed growth in the Manitoba Liberal Party's support. In Minto, Wayne Helgason improved the party's thirteen per cent showing in 2003 to thirty-one per cent. In Turtle Mountain, with Bev Leadbeater as the candidate, the party's support rose from eleven per cent in 2003 to nineteen per cent. Both results augur well for the future. In a Fort Whyte by-election in 2005, the party's support also increased.

Under Gerrard's leadership, the party is keeping to tradition, emphasizing responsible financial management and the creation of a compassionate and caring society. From an economic viewpoint, Gerrard follows in the footsteps of Greenway (with an emphasis on immigration), Campbell (on improving infrastructure and providing a strong climate for entrepreneurs and for business growth), Asper and Axworthy (in emphasizing the need to grow the economy by focusing on private sector investment and the creation of wealth), and of Carstairs (in recognizing the critical role of the provincial government to promote, together with Manitoba businesses, the research, development and innovation needed to generate new products and services).

Like Asper and Carstairs, Gerrard sees the level and nature of taxes as important to the location of enterprises and job growth. He supports the removal of the payroll tax, an NDP tax that has probably cost Manitoba tens of thousands of jobs as companies have moved elsewhere rather than grow in Manitoba. Sometimes, lowering a tax can over time bring in more provincial revenue because it results in more jobs and more economic growth.

Gerrard brings much to the table when it comes to fiscal management and economic development. As well as holding a degree in Economics, he worked closely with John Manley in Industry Canada and learned much from his time at the federal level during his time responsible for Science, Research and Development and Western Economic Diversification.

Like Carstairs, Gerrard is committed to a public system of health care, but sees the need to spend more wisely than we do today, and to provide much better management of the system than we have at the moment. Problems in health care are not solved solely by throwing more money at them. Keeping citizens healthy and preventing sickness is a vital part of the effort that is needed.

Gerrard is without a doubt the most knowledgeable leader when it comes to understanding health care. He recognizes the importance of building quality teams, and making changes to improve the quality of care and reduce costs. Changing processes to reduce errors is one such example. The challenge of the provincial government lies to a considerable extent in the approaches used to improving the overall health of Manitobans and in the approaches used to manage the quality and cost of health care. We can not short-change efforts to improve health. We also must not hesitate to make investments when they will improve quality while lowering the long-run operating costs.

Gerrard sees a strong commitment to environmental stewardship as critical to improving health and to improving our economic prosperity. Much economic benefit has been lost because fisheries on lakes like Lake Winnipegosis have been badly managed. Environmental damage creates costs to be borne by future generations just as surely as budget deficits do. Neither can be tolerated. In this respect, Gerrard brings his own strong background in environmental issues and follows clearly in the tradition of Liberals like Lloyd Axworthy, Harold Taylor and Terry Duguid. During his years in Ottawa, Gerrard co-chaired consultations on how to best assist and promote environmental industries. He understands the important role such businesses play in helping to maintain and improve our environment. His extensive work with bald eagles and other wildlife has also provided him with an in-depth knowledge of the boreal forest ecosystem.

When it comes to education, Gerrard follows in Carstairs' footsteps in the belief that quality is critical. He sees an important role in our schools for music, art and culture as well as for daily quality physical education. These areas have been shown to be significant in contributing to brain development and to learning. They also contribute to learning important life skills like discipline, ethics, communication, teamwork and the ability for creative expression. Gerrard also sees post-secondary education as vital.

When it comes to education finance, Gerrard follows Carstairs' lead in believing that eighty per cent of public education should be funded provincially. When it comes to the relationship between school boards and teachers, he follows the Campbell view that it's important to strike the right balance.

Like Norris, Asper and Carstairs, Gerrard is very concerned with issues surrounding Manitoba's underprivileged citizens. Decreasing poverty is fundamental to decreasing crime, improving health and increasing the productivity of Manitobans. Gerrard sees a need to overhaul the present approach to social assistance. His team has already outlined major changes to improve conditions for those with disabilities, and they are working to develop more effective approaches to decreasing the extent of poverty in Manitoba, which still has one of the highest rates of child poverty in Canada.

Like Greenway and Norris, Gerrard sees agriculture as one of Manitoba's fundamental industries. This is a province that is blessed with deep fertile soils and there are incredible opportunities in agriculture. Good health and good foods are closely linked and never more so than today as we move more into areas like higher value nutraceuticals and so-called "functional foods", which are associated with improvements in health.

Gerrard sees communities as vital. Governments can not

legislate how people interact in communities, but they can provide an environment to empower citizens to care for and to nourish their communities. In a global world, it is more important than ever that we are well rooted in our own communities, and are raised in an environment where we care for others and build societies in which individuals and families are nurtured.

When it comes to agriculture, Gerrard has been front and centre in looking at food safety and marketing issues. After the discovery of a cow with bovine spongiform encephalitis (BSE) in Canada, he called for testing of all cattle over thirty months of age to provide a guarantee of food safety and to improve farmers ability to market their cattle. Gerrard has also focused on asking such questions as: how do we decrease the risks to farmers? No longer is this just an issue of a better safety net, Manitoba must ensure farmers have adequate infrastructure, including good drainage, and the opportunity to use advances like tile drainage. Too much crop loss in recent years has resulted from inadequate attention to such basic infrastructure. Characteristic of his approach to issues generally, and to better understand water management issues like drainage and irrigation, Gerrard has spent many days in the field with knowledgeable farmers.

Aboriginal issues and the ability to work well with the federal government and with First Nations, Métis and Inuit leaders are very important to good provincial government. Gerrard has spent much time visiting First Nation and Métis communities and has, in each election, recruited candidates from the aboriginal community to ensure that the Manitoba Liberal Party will be able to deal with such issues well.

Following in the footsteps of Stuart Garson, Gerrard understands how important equalization transfers from the federal government have been to our province. At the same time, he recognizes the need for change. It's time for greater accountability. It is also time to recognize that equalization transfers must have a dual purpose, to provide a higher level of services to Manitobans, and also to help Manitoba to move from its current "have-not" status to the position of being a "have" province.

In considering justice issues, Gerrard is very much a follower of the views of Paul Edwards and Gary Kowalski. While he is firm on ensuring that there are consequences for those who commit crimes, he sees the importance of the provincial government in providing an environment where young people can thrive and a justice system that treats people fairly, for example making every effort to avoid wrongful convictions. In another example, the failure of the Tories and the NDP to provide a remand centre in Thompson has led to a brutal ferry service in which young and old offenders are forced to spend hours in incredibly cramped cells in vans as they are transported south to Winnipeg. Once there, young offenders from the north may be exposed to hardened criminals in a virtual "crime university". The chance to learn from their mistakes and turn their lives around is often lost.

As a physician, Gerrard is also concerned that mental health issues are often overlooked by the justice system. Recent estimates suggest as many as half of those in penal institutions may have mental health issues ranging from fetal alcohol syndrome to other forms of brain damage and mental disorder. Improving safety and decreasing criminal activity in Manitoba requires a new approach, focused on better communities, improved prevention and treatment of brain disorders. Better approaches to mental disorders can also help with other issues, including homelessness; a considerable proportion of those on the streets suffer from some form of mental illness.

In dealing with other issues, Gerrard is reflecting the changing nature of today's society. One area is in his understanding of the importance of cities to economic wealth and economic growth. A follower of Jane Jacobs, John Norquist and Richard Florida, Gerrard has read extensively on the nature of cities. He understands why it is so important to have liveable, growing cities where artistic activities, scientific discoveries and entrepreneurs can flourish. A child of the age of technology, he sees the critical role of information technology, biotechnology and environmental technology in helping us to deal with today's world, grow our province and create a better place to live.

In the 1999 provincial election, one of the most detailed policy documents released by the Manitoba Liberals concerned Winnipeg and the development of the mid-continent trade corridor. Gerrard spent a number of years during his medical training in Minneapolis and he and his family have lived for two six-month periods in Oklahoma City. He has driven the north-south mid-continent trade corridor many times, and he knows and understands its importance. This outward looking perspective is going to be crucial as Manitoba moves forward to take on the world.

It is in the context of becoming an important city of the world that Gerrard sees incredible opportunities for Winnipeg. Manitoba's major city has citizens from all corners of the globe and is therefore extraordinarily well positioned to interact and trade with the world. Winnipeg, through Folkorama and its many

Left: Jon with young people from Manto Sipi First Nation, who ran from Thompson to Winnipeg to gather support for improved recreation in their community ...

... and right, walking to raise awareness of Fetal Alcohol Syndrome ...

... taking part in a walk with Mr. and Mrs. Mohinder Singh, right, and joining members of the Manitoba Ethiopian Association at a demonstration in front of the Manitoba Legislature, below.

All photos on this page from the collection of Jon Gerrard

other cultural festivals, and through Canada's commitment to a society where people can retain their original languages, is positioned to do business anywhere in the world. Our goal now is to create the economic and social conditions that will further foster Winnipeg's global role.

The building of the Canadian Museum for Human Rights, the development of a boreal forest World Heritage Site, the creation of an international centre for aboriginal culture and an expansion of global trade and cultural links are all initiatives that Gerrard strongly supports. In short, Gerrard has the background and skills to be premier. The unanswered question is whether Manitoba voters will decide to put their trust and hopes in his leadership.

CONCLUSION

M ANITOBANS CAN TAKE PRIDE in the traditions and history of the Liberal Party in Manitoba. Between 1888 and 1958, four Liberal premiers served for a combined total of thirty-four years and provided many of the critical building blocks that make Manitoba what it is today. Add to that ten years of a coalition government during the 1930s, and many years in opposition, and it is clear the Liberal Party has helped this province grow.

None of those Liberal premiers was chased from office by scandal or criminal activity and every one of those Liberal governments demonstrated strong fiscal responsibility, managing to improve services while spending smarter. This record sets Manitoba's Liberal governments apart from their Conservative and NDP counterparts, many of which have shown either poor social or poor economic management.

Throughout Manitoba's history, Liberals have emphasized compassion for those in need, a strong sense of balance and fairness in government and the economy, and a progressive, innovative, and forward-thinking vision for the future of the province. Manitoba Liberals, the keystone party in our Keystone Province, have contributed much.

The last forty-six years have seen Manitoba slide from being a leader to a slower-growing have-not province. Health care costs are high, yet service is low, and we cannot retain enough nurses and doctors to fill our needs. Universities are suffering from decades of funding cuts, roads are crumbling, and in recent decades the idea of a strong economy seems to be either expanding the public sector or subsidizing industry. Manitoba's economy and population have grown much less than the rest of many parts of Canada.

We have an incredible province with huge potential. It is time we sought to reach that potential. Gerrard believes the Manitoba Liberal Party can change this slide, demonstrating through actions, not campaign slogans, the character, vision and values necessary to guide our province to a better future. He and I believe that Manitoba needs a Liberal government. We hope that those who read this book will agree, and take their own steps to help make our better future possible.

Courtesy of Jon Gerrard

With Jon Gerrard, these youngsters—(left to right) Emma, Chanelle and Heather McKenzie—seem to be saying the sky's the limit for future Liberals.

11

The Future

Every time I rise to speak in the Manitoba Legislature, I am physically reminded where the Manitoba Liberals stand in provincial politics. My seat in the legislature is positioned too close to the desk in front, and as I speak, the chair digs into my calves. Many MLAs move their chairs to the right or left to ensure a comfortable stance, but for me, this is not an option. It is not easy standing like this, but I do it to show anyone who may look that I am in the middle—I am not tilting right or left. Liberals are neither NDP nor Conservatives.

When I moved into provincial politics in 1998, I had other options. I could have spent the rest of my working career as a practicing physician caring for children with blood problems and cancer. I would have been immersed in a comfortable occupation for which I was trained, and I would have been assured of a substantial income and more than adequate time for vacations with my family.

Instead, I chose to enter provincial politics. I knew the hours would be long, the pay would be less, and the goal of influencing provincial political decisions and achieving a provincial Liberal government would certainly be difficult.

My decision did not come easily.

Some cynical people thought my reasons for entering provincial politics were to get a Senate seat or some other appointment. They were and still are wrong. My sole interest is in representing people as an elected official. I knew that this decision would make it unlikely I would ever return to federal politics, but I also knew that the future of Manitoba lies much more in the hands of provincial elected officials than in the hands of federal elected officials. MPs will always have to provide approaches which balance the interests of all provinces. This is not to say that federal decisions are not important. They are. This is not to say that federal decisions do not have an impact. They do. But whether Manitoba succeeds or fails, whether it prospers or declines, is primarily in the hands of those who are elected provincially.

Manitoba currently benefits enormously from federal equalization payments and from federal cash transfers for areas including health, social services, post-secondary education, and infrastructure. But the way in which these dollars are spent, and how health care, education, infrastructure and social services are managed, are decisions made almost exclusively at the provincial level.

I also felt strongly that it was time to bridge the rural-urban divide. For the most part, I have lived in rural Manitoba and I represented a rural region, federally. But cities are today's economic engines, and safe, diverse, forward-thinking cities are vital to the future.

Being a Manitoba politician is, of course, not solely about the well-being of our own province. We are the keystone province, and we have a role to hold our wonderful country together, to shape and develop it. Nowhere is this more critical than in the nurturing of the French language and francophone culture in Manitoba. Ties between our francophone community and those in Québec and in other provinces are vital for us to maintain. Respecting and ensuring continuity to the French language and francophone culture in Manitoba are essential to ensuring respect and continuity for the many different cultures and languages in our province. And it's not only important at home; it's critical to our potential to work and trade with others around the world, and to build a global presence for Manitoba.

Though English was our language at home when I was growing up, my years in Montréal have enabled me to communicate in French. All our children, through French immersion programs, are bilingual. I believe that provincial leaders with a capacity to speak French will be an important part of our future to keep Canada whole.

In making my decision to enter provincial politics in 1998, I had the advantage of having traveled extensively across Canada, and of observing how things were managed in other provinces. I also had the advantage of visiting other countries as the minister responsible for Science in Canada, and of talking with many people about the role of science, research and technology in improving health care, the environment and social services, as well as in building the economy.

I have still had much to learn about provincial politics. And writing this book has certainly given me a better understanding of the past successes and failures of the provincial Liberal Party.

The Manitoba Liberal Party was in government for thirty-five years between 1888 and 1958. While Liberal governments have not been without their defects, they have been good governments for Manitoba, free from major scandals and free from overspending.

Greenway cut the costs of the machinery of provincial government by forty per cent. Norris, in more difficult times economically, brought in a government that introduced an improved understanding of fairness, responsibility, and accountability in the wake of the financing scandal surrounding the building of the Legislature under Rodmund Roblin. Garson successfully negotiated a fairer financing package from the federal government, the forerunner of Manitoba's equalization transfers from Ottawa. Campbell was well known for his care and wisdom in making expenditures and for his tough but fair negotiations. When International Nickel came to develop the mine in northern Manitoba, he emphasized that they came not because of a government subsidy, but because they saw a good business opportunity.

The Liberal tradition in Manitoba is for government to invest wisely and improve our life, particularly by improving democracy and provincial governance.

Liberal principles start from a fundamental respect for the freedom and dignity of the individual. A Liberal society is first and foremost one where basic human rights and civil liberties—such as freedom of expression and belief, due legal process, democratic participation—are guaranteed for all citizens. Moreover, Manitoba's affirming brand of positive liberalism emphasizes that collective assistance may be necessary for individuals to fully exercise their rights as citizens. Greenway ended the ability of people to vote in more than one constituency and introduced one man one vote. Norris, in 1915, ensured the provincial franchise for women. Campbell corrected another injustice and extended the vote to aboriginal people in Manitoba in the 1950s. First Nation and Métis people remain important to the party, which has made a determined effort to reach out to the community. Seven of the fifty-seven Liberal candidates in 2003 were aboriginal.

A Liberal government will always ensure that Manitobans have basic human rights to quality education and health care, housing for those in need, and respect for the young and the elderly. Liberal values of religious and cultural tolerance were principal reasons for encouraging Mennonites to come to Manitoba when they faced persecution in Russia, and have been important in supporting those who come more recently as refugees fearing harassment, torture or death in their own countries.

Liberal governments have been visionary, innovative and activist. Greenway and Clifford Sifton led a vast tide of immigration into the province. The Norris government became the very centre of reform activity in Canada from 1915-1922. Garson was the father of equalization transfers. Douglas Campbell led the way in bringing electricity to Manitoba.

Liberals know the importance of fostering a culture of entrepreneurship, and of providing an optimum and productive balance in the interests of workers and entrepreneurs. Liberals are strong supporters of using market mechanisms as an efficient and responsive way of organizing production and distributing the economic bounty of our province. Liberals also know that all well-functioning markets require a public infrastructure, clearly-defined rules around property and the workplace, and laws to ensure fairness and creative competition. But Liberals also understand that basic fairness requires government to step in when necessary to make sure the economy works for all Manitobans, not just the powerful, the wealthy or any other segment of society.

Our progressive brand of Liberalism sees the role of government as ensuring that every Manitoban has both the opportunity and the means to contribute to society. Liberals see the contributions of scientists and research as important "candles" to light the way of social and human progress. Liberals see the gifts of artists and architects, writers and engineers as vital to creating an environment where citizens can lead healthy and productive lives. Liberals see the potential of communities to build a better future for Manitobans.

Attention to infrastructure has been a strong feature of

Liberal governments. Greenway was very concerned about the development of the railways and rail infrastructure. He also paid a lot of attention to drainage infrastructure for farmers. Norris was involved in the development of plans for the railway to the Hudson Bay. Campbell oversaw a major expansion of the highway system in Manitoba. He also established the commission that was the catalyst for building the Winnipeg Floodway, though the floodway itself was not constructed until the next decade.

Our party's brand of liberalism emphasizes the responsibility of citizens to demonstrate compassion and fair play. Norris brought in social and labour legislation such as workmen's compensation, a minimum wage, an industrial relations act, and an allowance for widowed dependent mothers. In the 1950s, Campbell introduced legislation that lasted forty years, providing the basis for fair bargaining between teachers and school boards.

Liberals are diverse and broad-minded, open to new ideas that challenge tradition, established institutions, and conventional ways of thinking. Liberal principles emphasize a government which gives opportunity to every citizen to express their talents, skills and ability; a liberal society is one that provides the individual with both space (personal liberty) and support (government action) for the full flowering of the human spirit.

We live in a time when three separate revolutions are changing our world. These revolutions provide economic opportunities but government must be open, transparent and accountable.

There is a revolution in computers, information systems and the Internet. There is a revolution in our approach to the environment and to building a sustainable world. Resources are limited, and wastes—solid, liquid or greenhouse gases—can no longer be produced and discarded.

There is a revolution in our approach to biotechnology and molecular biology. Extraordinary advances have been made in genetics and in understanding and being able to modify the DNA which makes up our genes. This revolution has tremendous potential for good, but also raises significant concerns about the misuse of this knowledge.

These revolutions are changing the relationship among citizens, government and the environment. Liberals look at the long-term picture for Manitoba. Critical to our view is our commitment to leaving future Manitobans with an environment that is healthier and more sustainable than the one we inherited. Liberals see injury to the environment as unfair and unacceptable deficit spending—the unloading of current costs and impacts from one generation onto the next. Liberals are adamant that government has a responsibility to ensure that environmental values are properly reflected in the actions and affairs of individuals, economic operations, communities and government itself.

We see ourselves as guardians of the future, ensuring that today's businesses and consumers are internalizing the costs of their activities rather than being subsidized by future generations. Our environment sustains us and enriches us economically aesthetically, recreationally, culturally, historically, and spiritually. We recognize that we are an integral part of nature, and destruction of the environment harms Manitoba society today and in the future.

Understanding the developments arising from these three technological revolutions allows us to advance the nature of government, to build our economy, to improve our health and to protect our environment all at the same time.

Before I entered politics, too many inadequate provincial decisions convinced me that the Liberal party could provide better choices and vision than the NDP or Conservatives. Manitoba, well governed, has an incredible future. Good stewardship of our present hydro-electric power resources coupled with wise development of new sites can give us a solid foundation. I see huge potential in the growth of medical and biotechnology, and environmental technology. As the centre of the North American continent, I see prospects for Winnipeg and Manitoba in trucking, aerospace and telecommunications. Our agricultural base can be built into a powerhouse for developing, growing and processing crops with improved health benefits—crops that will be increasingly in demand.

I see huge potential in global exports facilitated by our diverse population, fluent in many of the world's languages, and sensitive to cultures around the world. I see a large potential to attract young people, with fresh ideas and new ways of thinking. I see the contributions of First Nation, Métis and Inuit Manitobans anchoring a marriage of old wisdom and twenty-first century dreams. As Grand Chief Phil Fontaine explained recently on CBC Radio, declining birthrates among non-aboriginal Canadians and rising birthrates in the aboriginal communities may mean that Canada will be relying in the future on an increasingly aboriginal workforce to make Canada work.

Manitoba stands at the threshold of opportunity. If we draw on the strength and courage of those men and women who changed our lives because of their passion for a better world, the

Courtesy of Jon Gerrard

Jon Gerrard enjoys the beauty of Manitoba's Assiniboine River with Betsy Burt.

future is ours to embrace. Unearthing their voyage of discovery has been a new journey in itself. There was much to learn, and this book is the result of that learning.

Appendix

An April 30, 1959 memo to candidates from J.F. Sullivan, chairman of the Manitoba Liberal-Progessive Election Committee, provides an interesting perspective on the thinking within the Liberal Party:

The following are suggestions which you may use, if you like.

1. Liberals stand for a sane, practical policy of paying for current expenditures out of current revenue and borrowing for capital construction on a sound, repayable basis, thus avoiding tax increases and sales tax.

2. Liberals established the hospital insurance plan through the co-operation of federal and provincial governments. Liberals stand for the extension of the social insurance principle into the medical and dental fields, not on the basis of state medicine, but by the implementation of a major medical benefit plan. A resolution along these lines was adopted unanimously at our last annual meeting.

3. Our Party stands for true equality of educational opportunity …

4. [Section deals in essence with local school division autonomy in decision making.]

5. Liberal Progressives have always advocated respect for constituted authorities and particular municipal governing bodies. We do not think it is any of the business of the Premier of Manitoba to tell a city where its city hall should be. Respect for municipal authority is vital to a proper functioning of our province.

6. Liberals stand for fair treatment of every constituency regardless of political stripe. We regard as contrary to our traditions the suggestions being made by Tory candidates that road and bridges should be denied to those constituencies which elect an Opposition member.

7. Merit rating for teachers was a positive recommendation of the Royal Commission on Education. The Royal Commission urged merit rating as an essential accompaniment of larger school units. Roblin has side-stepped this issue. Our caucus has declared for merit rating.

8. Liberal Progressives if returned to office, would continue the Liberal road improvement programs which Roblin has followed. Our policy has been to work for the greatest mileage of roads for the greatest number of people. Now that the Trans-Canada highway is nearing completion, money can be used for city and town access roads and through streets, and for market roads.

9. Dominion-Provincial relations may not have a direct vote appeal but they are vital to a continuation of Manitoba's progress …

10. The agricultural problems of Manitoba require understanding and consideration from provincial leaders …

11. Television in the north is ridiculed by the Tories, but it can be brought into effect—not by the province usurping federal jurisdiction, but with a Liberal-Progressive government in Manitoba giving a lead. Some said rural electrification was a pipe dream, but it is now a reality. So can television for outlying parts of Manitoba be a reality.

12. We will continue to develop the tourist trade …

13. We will continue to develop the North …

14. A higher minimum wage is in keeping with the changing economy. This was the stand adopted by an overwhelming majority at our annual meeting. Liberal-Progressives are sympathetic to responsible trade unions. We advocate a full time Minister of Labour.

15. Duplication of services in the long run can only add to the expense of the services.

16. Liberals generally accept the idea that license fees should cover costs and should not be used for revenue because that amounts to indirect taxation …

17. Liberals look with favour on the adoption of a Physical Fitness and Recreational Program as recommended by the Commission on Recreation.